D0141148

Social Work and Disadvantage

by the same author

Brothers and Sisters of Disabled Children
Peter Burke
ISBN 1 84310 043 6

of related interest

Social Capital and Mental Health
Edited by Kwame McKenzie and Trudy Harpham
ISBN 1 84310 355 9

Dementia and Social Inclusion
Marginalised Groups and Marginalised Areas of Dementia Research,
Care and Practice
Edited by Anthea Innes, Carole Archibald and Charlie Murphy
ISBN 1 84310 174 2

Drug Addiction and Families
Marina Barnard
ISBN 1 84310 403 2

'Race', Housing and Social Exclusion
Edited by Peter Somerville and Andy Steele
ISBN 1 85302 849 5

Deportation is Freedom!
The Orwellian World of Immigration Controls
Steve Cohen
ISBN 1 84310 294 3

Working with Parents of Young People
Research, Policy and Practice
Edited by Debi Roker and John Coleman
ISBN 1 84310 420 2

Special Stories for Disability Awareness
Stories and Activities for Teachers, Parents and Professionals
Mal Leicester
ISBN 1 84310 390 7

Introducing Mental Health
A Practical Guide
Caroline Kinsella and Connor Kinsella
ISBN 1 84310 260 9

Social Work and Disadvantage

Addressing the Roots of Stigma
Through Association

Edited by Peter Burke and Jonathan Parker

Jessica Kingsley Publishers
London and Philadelphia

First published in 2007
by Jessica Kingsley Publishers
116 Pentonville Road
London N1 9JB, UK
and
400 Market Street, Suite 400
Philadelphia, PA 19106, USA

www.jkp.com

Copyright © Jessica Kingsley Publishers 2007

The right of the contributors to be identified as authors of this work has been asserted by
them in accordance with the Copyright, Designs and Patents Act 1988.

All rights reserved. No part of this publication may be reproduced in any material form
(including photocopying or storing it in any medium by electronic means and whether or not
transiently or incidentally to some other use of this publication) without the written
permission of the copyright owner except in accordance with the provisions of the
Copyright, Designs and Patents Act 1988 or under the terms of a licence issued by the
Copyright Licensing Agency Ltd, 90 Tottenham Court Road, London, England W1T 4LP.
Applications for the copyright owner's written permission to reproduce any part of this
publication should be addressed to the publisher.

Warning: The doing of an unauthorised act in relation to a copyright work may result in both
a civil claim for damages and criminal prosecution.

Library of Congress Cataloging in Publication Data
Social work and disadvantage : addressing the roots of stigma through association / edited
by Peter Burke and Jonathan Parker.
p. cm.
Includes bibliographical references and index.
ISBN-13: 978-1-84310-364-6 (pbk.)
ISBN-10: 1-84310-364-8 (pbk.)
1. Social work with people with disabilities. 2. Sociology of disability. 3. Stigma (Social
psychology) I. Burke, Peter, 1948- II. Parker, Jonathan, 1960-
HV1568.S696 2007
361.3'2--dc22

2006019502

British Library Cataloguing in Publication Data
A CIP catalogue record for this book is available from the British Library

ISBN-13: 978 1 84310 364 6
ISBN-10: 1 84310 364 8

Printed and bound in Great Britain by
Athenaeum Press, Gateshead, Tyne and Wear

Contents

Figures

Tables

Introduction

Peter Burke and Jonathan Parker

The book examines disadvantage as an associative condition in social work. The topic of disadvantage originally related to research by Burke and Montgomery (2003) which mainly concerned the siblings of disabled children, and led to the more detailed exposition in *Brothers and Sisters of Disabled Children* (Burke, 2004) in which the concept of disability by association is introduced. This text builds on the concept of 'disability by association' but broadens its grasp to reflect the sense of disadvantage experienced across a spectrum of client and user groups, and explores the potential for the positive requisition of association as a way of understanding and working with others.

In expanding this, we have drawn on the expertise of professional colleagues and, although this extends the original concept, it is not an exhaustive examination, but sufficient to reflect the transferability of the concept to other areas of academic interest, research and practice. In providing an examination of disadvantage, the areas we cover include childhood disability as an origination source, but we also explore in some detail the stigma of association in a much wider-ranging set of experiences. The text includes children in the looked after system, their families, drug users, HIV/AIDS, issues of sexuality for older people and age-related disabilities. In all these areas, the question of associated issues relating to an initiating condition is addressed.

The need for social workers to be highly skilled and knowledgeable about the consequences of practice is a basic imperative within the profession. Social work education has undergone a major transformation to ensure that qualified social workers understand the complexities of the human condition, and this is reflected by the requirements set by the Department of Health (2002). The changes are further stressed in the Assessment Framework utilised in child care, the developments heralded by *Every Child Matters* (Chief Secretary to the Treasurer, 2003), *Valuing People* (Department of

Health, 2001) and in the White Paper *Our Health, Our Care, Our Say* (Department of Health, 2006), which together identify the centrality of the individual experiencing some degree of need within the systems of social care. The complexity of social relations feature too, such that any objective assessment of individual need must also consider the impact on others within the systemic framework in which that individual lives; in conceptualising this extension we enter the genre of associative conditions.

Social workers work with people who are vulnerable, who are struggling in some way to participate fully in society. In essence, we focus on current practice and research-informed knowledge to develop a generalisable model of associative conditions that transfer across a variety of social care settings. The basic model is open to further evaluation; the examinations made do not cover all possible situations, although the relevance to many indicates some potential for the particular.

It would appear that the sense of disadvantage that distinguishes many individuals on the receiving end of social work is associated with perceptions of need, identified by location, attitudes and barriers to change. These structural issues and the stigmatisation of disadvantage are examined in some detail. We will now outline the book's organisation.

Outline of chapters

Chapter 1, by Peter Burke, provides a theoretical background to the subsequent chapters, which in turn review the research evidence that links to the experience of those encountering disadvantage through associative interactions.

In Chapter 2 Catherine Deverell examines the experience of children in the care system and reveals disadvantage and stigma associated with the child's experience and background.

Peter Burke and Benedict Fell, in Chapter 3, introduce further research on the family examining issues for children with disabilities and the consequences for siblings. This extends the research by Burke (2004) to show that siblings experience disability as part of their lives and carry a social identity that incorporates a sense of disability as though they shared the disability of their brother or sister.

In Chapter 4 Philip Guy discusses drug use and the impact on the family. It is suggested that this family dimension is often overlooked, indeed undervalued, in considerations of the consequences of living with a drug user. Families, it seems, are indeed stigmatised by association with a drug user.

Chapter 5, by Liz Walker, looks at the issues raised by HIV/AIDS in South Africa and explores the consequences of caring for people living with HIV/AIDS. Research was conducted with community-based volunteers that demonstrated how 'transmitted deprivation' might be interrupted.

Elizabeth Price, in Chapter 6, turns to issues of ageing for gay men and lesbians. She undertakes an exploration which reveals that stigma is not only attributed to socially held attitudes to growing older, a feature that becomes identifiable with the over 65s in the UK, but that the associated stigma – of also being gay in an apparently heterosexual community – adds to the experience of disadvantage. The associative element of sexual orientation further compounds a negative stereotypical view of ageing in contemporary society.

In Chapter 7, Jonathan Parker examines contemporary social work practice with people who experience dementia and explores the current context as social work and social care moves into multidimensional aspects of practice. A critique arising from labelling and deviance theory and drawing upon disadvantage by association helps explain the context in which social work with people with dementia needs to to extend professional boundaries.

Margaret Holloway uses her research evidence to inform Chapter 8, and examines the experience of living with Parkinson's disease, providing clear evidence that indicates that the stigma associated with Parkinson's disease has a very real impact on the immediate family and carers. The experience of living with chronic illness is demonstrated as having a spiralling effect as debility increases and carers find it harder and harder to manage their daily lives.

In Chapter 9, Jonathan Parker reflects on the full spectrum effect of anti-oppressive practice. The concept and theory of anti-oppressive practice is identified as a necessary cornerstone to social work practice in the UK; a model for good practice in social work is developed.

In the concluding chapter, Peter Burke brings together a number of reflections to reframe our understanding of disadvantage and stigma of associative conditions and to suggest that some realignment of the assessment framework is necessary to extend beyond the needs of the individual and to incorporate themes developed throughout this book.

This text is intended to improve our understanding of the stigmatisation process, embedded with the disadvantage of associated conditions and applied to the social care practitioner. We would like to ensure that practitioners working with those on the receiving end of disadvantaged experiences will see, in the chapters within this book, that an attempt has been made to understand them and to improve our knowledge base in this area.

This book cannot and should not be thought to clarify any but a minority of experiences, but it should, nevertheless, show that the issue of associative disadvantage pervades the social structure with which social care professionals engage, and as such should be helpful in informing practice. In order to make changes it is necessary to recognise the problems faced by service users and their families, and to take into account the consequences of this conceptualisation of associative disadvantage, in formulating and enriching practice.

References

Burke, P. (2004) *Brothers and Sisters of Disabled Children*. London: Jessica Kingsley Publishers.

Burke, P. and Montgomery, S. (2003) *Finding a Voice: Expanding Horizons in Social Work and Allied Professions*. Birmingham: Ventura Press.

Chief Secretary to the Treasurer (2003) *Every Child Matters*. Cm 5860. London: The Stationery Office.

Department of Health (2001) *Valuing People: A New Strategy for Learning Disability for the 21st Century*. London: The Stationery Office.

Department of Health (2002) *Requirements for the Training of Social Workers*. London: Department of Health.

Department of Health (2006) *Our Health, Our Care, Our Say*. London: Department of Health.

Chapter 1

Disadvantage and Stigma: A Theoretical Framework for Associated Conditions

Peter Burke

The title of this book embraces the need to reappraise social work of the fundamental consequence of disadvantage. A definition of 'disadvantage' favoured by the Department of Work and Pensions (2005) concerns 'multiple' disadvantage in the labour market and includes 'the over 50s, lone parents, disabled, ethnic and / or those with no or low skills' (press release 1 October 2005). Graham and Power (2004) discuss disadvantage as the transmission of worsening inequalities from generation to generation through economic, social and development processes that are reinforced in adult life. Hence, disadvantage extends beyond the economic to the social and developmental aspects of health. The term 'disadvantage' is used in an inclusive sense, and is viewed as a factor that permeates the experience of many people who, perhaps not through choice, are vulnerable or stigmatised, or are in other ways incapacitated in their dealings with the situations and experiences of everyday life.

This chapter shows, as the book will testify, how certain groups of people, who experience disadvantage in any number of ways, become stigmatised in their relationships with others. Stigma will be seen as a key element in disadvantage and it exists within a number of different arenas. Once a person experiences the difference of not being equal to others, whether physically, sexually, financially, intellectually or in any other way, they become invisibly labelled as not being a member of the same mainstream as the majority. This is the impact of stigma. Stigma may represent a stereotypical view of certain groups of people, whether of a particular gender or persuasion, and has the potential to isolate and exclude them from social relationships with others. These experiences are marked by a sense of inequality, impoverishment and failure that may lead to the experience of social exclusion.

The transferability of disadvantage as a quantity will be underpinned by an examination of stigma and the commensurate qualities it imposes. The fact of disadvantage will be viewed as having a stigmatising effect, so that association with groups who are perceived as disadvantaged will carry disadvantage as a form of secondary experience: associating with disadvantaged groups or individuals confers an element of disadvantage on the associate. The experience of living with associative disadvantage and the stigma that is experienced are factors that will be examined in the chapters that follow. The root of this conceptualisation of stigmatisation lies within my work on childhood disability and the impact that disability has on brothers and sisters within the family (Burke, 2004) to suggest that non-disabled siblings perceive themselves as disabled by the fact of having a family member who has a disabling impairment.

It may seem strange then, that the chapters presented in this book, which deal with associative conditions, do not look at the detailed lives of individuals who are central to the experience of disadvantage to any significant degree but, instead, examine the situation of those people who are in some way linked with the disadvantaged person. This is deliberate; it is not intended to diminish the needs of disadvantaged individuals, but to comment on the negative associative power of their situation as reflected by the experience of others with whom they are in regular contact. The anti-social experience of discrimination is, by its invasive nature, behaviour that touches all but those who actively discriminate; it is, in the context of those experiencing such effects, a form of oppression that must not be accepted. The need addressed in this text is to counter the impact of those who are discriminated against – whether they are individuals, family members or professionals – to level such experiences as identified through an associative order and to eradicate such discrimination as might be experienced. This in turn points to a role for the social work practitioner.

However, in order to orientate the reader within a framework of disadvantage, stigma and its associative conditions, it is necessary to explore the component parts of this conceptualisation in their relationship to each other. This will help the reader to understand the concept of disability by association within its wider framework of social disadvantage.

A framework of social disadvantage

The concept of social disadvantage is indicative, as Graham and Power (2004) would attest, that some individuals do not go through life with the same good fortune as others. Indeed the sense of disadvantage captured by a sense of 'good fortune' may extend beyond the individual to some communities, ethnic and minority groups that do not share the same opportunities as other groups. And while some seem to experience 'bad fortune', it might be that a form of oppression constructs such experiences from a state of 'multiple disadvantage' due to implacable barriers to furthering achievement.

'Deprivation' is consequently a term that is linked with disadvantage to indicate that disadvantage is produced by the exclusion from some commodity, service or opportunity. It may refer to a range of experience of deprivation that builds to a disadvantaged state. Abercrombie, Hill and Turner (2000) suggest a 'cycle of deprivation' whereby failure to provide adequate parenting leads to poor child rearing; child deprivation results, with intellectual and social deficits, followed by unskilled jobs or unemployment and, subsequently, unsatisfying marriages. Poverty may well be a factor in a failure to provide a culturally rich and healthy environment, leading to long-term consequences for those on the lower rungs of society, such that structural impairments within our society result in groups that are labelled and identified as disadvantaged.

McGhee and Waterhouse (2002) indicate that poverty leads to family disruption and poor health in both parents and child, and would contribute to the cycle of deprivation reported by Abercrombie *et al.* (2000). Individuals within disadvantaged groups who experience poverty should not carry the blame for their condition any more than an individual with an impairment should be blameworthy for being different. It appears to be the case that some do not have equality of opportunity and cannot avail themselves of the same degree of achievement as others. This is not just about elements of luck and good fortune. Sir Keith Joseph, in the oft-quoted speech of 1972, raised the issue of employment opportunity when he asked: 'Why is it that, in spite of long periods of full employment and relative prosperity...deprivation and problems of maladjustment so conspicuously persist?' (Joseph, in Denham and Garnet, 2002: 193). The issue of persistent disadvantage that equates with deprivation and problems of adjustment suggests that disadvantage and lack of opportunity are not necessarily problems for the individual to resolve but reflect on societal values and situational opportunities. This means that, depending on a particular geographical location, where you live and how schools, training and work experiences are sought either enable a reduction of deprivation and social disorder or encourage a sense of difference and disadvantage.

The common parlance of social deprivation reflected in Sir Keith Joseph's message is of persistent disadvantage to the undeserving, which is victim blaming, and is reinforced by the media, frequently in the housing and employment market, utilising terms like 'the North–South divide'. The persistence of deprivation, however, is suggestive, rather as indicated in the Abercrombie *et al.* thesis (2000), that the fabric of social structure is somehow to blame rather than an individualistic model of inadequacy located within the family. A causal explanation might suggest that both are linked, that poverty is a constituent contributor to individual and familial failure.

According to Rutter and Madge (1976) while deprivation is linked to environmental forces, disadvantage is also part of discrimination; in particular, this has been represented by the experience of 'black' people in this country. Parker (1971) had already shown that black children were likely to be deprived and underprivileged given a life experience that reflected higher than average rates of illegitimacy, corresponding low levels of educational opportunity, and living in areas of relative poverty. Discrimination then became an active force that stereotyped individuals by an association of colour, low-level education expectations and a life of poverty in areas of housing deprivation. Discrimination and deprivation appear to lead to disadvantage; indeed, there seems be a causal linking between them despite their being a social construction. Cheetham (1982) suggests that low-level expectations associated with disadvantage typify people in a negative sense that fails to recognise the strength of unity in black families. The need is not to blame individuals for their situational experiences (i.e. where they live), but to recognise what might well be a triumph of unity over adversity, in the adjustment to a quality of life under disadvantaged circumstances.

In this sense disadvantage is viewed as a socially constructed concept. The majority of disadvantages are due to situational factors which serve to judge individuals in a negative sense rather than recognising people whose investment in family life is focused on making their lives socially and economically better. An explanation of why differential perceptions exist in viewing social structures is found in the literature on cultural difference and the rise of conflicts: Banks (1991) comments on cultural misunderstanding as being due to a sense of difference between minority cultural belief systems existing within the framework of majority cultural expectations. Yang and McMullen's (2003) research shows that learning about other cultures may help us to improve our understanding of cultural differences. The failure to recognise difference envelops a protective barrier of exclusion, which discourages any attempt at understanding. If a situation is not understood, it is easier to ignore it than to challenge its foundation.

Barnes and Mercer (2003: 9) seem to identify the point of imposition when referring to Hunt (1966) on the 'suffering' experienced by disabled people and how the impact of impairment intervenes in our relationships with 'normal' people. Disability in this context is set aside from the ordinary, resulting in oppression and discrimination. Once again, oppression and discrimination conspire towards a situation of disadvantage. This fits with the circumstances of families who experience normality themselves but feel oppressed and discriminated against should they be associated with a disabled child or sibling.

Difference in this example is between the culture of 'normality' and 'disability' in a world that encourages social inclusion but where individual experience denies its reality. This example only identifies a possible explanation for a small sequence of events that 'fear' difference. However, the accumulation of numerous such events, involving day-to-day interactions, gives credence to the stereotypical image of disability and the avoidance by non-identifiable group members.

In a sense, this is a reflection of the argument that Lee and Loveridge (1987) recount in the manufacture of disadvantage, where they question the values that underpin the experience of social deprivation. The values result in stigmatisation because hierarchical exchanges promote a sense that is less than acceptance, or, to express it another way, the feeling is of being deprived of 'normality'. It is important, therefore, to explore the basis of stigma in its constructional sense, building on the elements of interactions to show whether one group typifies another due to an apparent condition in which the stereotype may exist. Such interactions appear to be based on race, gender, education, intellectual ability or not, or some other characteristic such as weight, height and appearance.

Stigma

It may be that certain individuals are predisposed to behave in a particular way and that biological inheritances will influence the development of personality, whether related to inherited characteristics of intelligence (Eysenck, 1971), or behaviourally linking early experience of parental nurturing (Bowlby, 1971). Indeed, nutritional problems of limitation or excess lead to later life effects including predispositions to early mortality (Blackwell et al., 2001; Graham and Power, 2004). Even the impact of income differentials on child development has raised issues, although the research is inconclusive (Jenkins and Schluter, 2002).

Human nature might seem to some degree to have elements of predetermination, but the issue for social scientists is about how people make choices and their latitude to do so wherever their natural inheritance and early life experiences might lead them. Stigma is the associative condition that predisposes people towards set attitudes, which, rather than being biologically driven, reflect the continuation of socialising (or perhaps un-socialising) experiences and then feature as a form of discrimination against certain identifiable groups of people.

Stigma has many definitions. The following quotation from the New Freedom Commission on Mental Health concerns the impact of mental disorder, which is interpreted within its broader context, and defines stigma thus:

> Stigma refers to a cluster of negative attitudes and beliefs that motivate the general public to fear, reject, avoid, and discriminate against people with mental illnesses. Stigma is widespread in the United States and other Western nations. Stigma leads others to avoid living, socializing, or working with, renting to, or employing people with mental disorders – especially severe disorders, such as schizophrenia. It leads to low self-esteem, isolation, and hopelessness. (Hogan, 2003)

It is clear from the above definition that stigma concerns interactions that are, in part, painful. If we take the question of avoidance, for example, the simple avoidance of social contact in the street or in a social setting with a previously known individual serves to accentuate a sense of difference in the individual perceiving the rejection or may be viewed as a fear of association by the individual perpetuating the rejection.

Stigma is clearly a combination of factors, depending on the position of one's perception. For the purposes of this book stigma can be analysed within three areas representing the unique quality of individual experiences:

- *social* – how others treat you in day-to-day interactions/ self-realisation

- *situational* – how location and place impact on individual identity

- *structural* – how people in authority treat you (doctors, teachers and officials).

These stigmatising interactions are represented in Figure 1.1. This shows that the impact of stigma may have the potential to create an experience of social exclusion as the cumulative effect of such experiences. It is apparent from Figure 1.1 that the experience of social exclusion may result from a position of disadvantage that is reinforced by social, situational or structural aspects of stigmatisation. The process of social exclusion arises from these experiences occurring within everyday interactions. However, Figure 1.1 only represents those who are stigmatised directly; it does not necessarily represent any associative elements of identifying with, knowing or working with a stigmatised individual. The process of association, which labels the individual who is linked in some way with the experience of those who are stigmatised, extends the potential for social exclusion, as though tainted in some way by the experience of being in the company of a stigmatised individual.

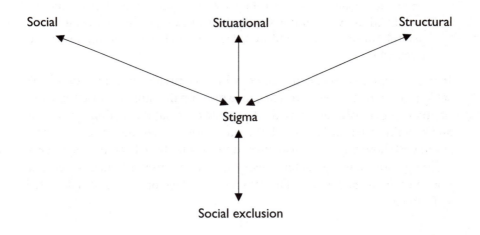

Figure 1.1 The experience of disadvantage

Social aspects of stigma

The social aspect of stigma is clarified by Goffman (1963) who suggests that some groups of people are not treated in the same way as others and will exist on the margins of society. Such experiences lead these individuals to have a devalued status. In Goffman's accounts they may be represented by those who are labelled mentally ill; other stigmatised groups may include those in minority groups or people who are identified as ex-convicts and, of course, those who have certain types of disabilities. Stigma carries the sense of not being true to culturally desired norms of behaviour, and consequently such people have what Goffman calls a 'spoiled identity'.

Goffman (1974: 56) described disabling conditions as stigmatising in a similar way; that is, when specific behaviours do not conform to the expectations of others. The consequence is that a negative reaction is evoked and the individual experiences this as a form of punishment. The pressure is to conform to a type that is 'socially accepted', rather than accepting individuals as they are. Clearly, an individual whose status cannot be changed by conforming will experience continued stigmatisation by others: this is the social experience of stigma.

Paul Toh (2004) from the Health and Development Network (HDN), working with UNAIDS in Thailand following his diagnosis in a foreign country, explains how stigma can be self-assigning. This is an internalised form of social stigma. He writes:

> My own personal experience is totally one of myself, fighting my self-stigmatisation. No one discriminated against me; it was me who discriminated against myself, creating a stigma splitting my personality into two. I had to live with this situation for three years before I made a very painful but determined and firm decision to change, and the result was tremendous.

It is apparent that social pressures, which combine with an individual's self-perception, may result in a negative reaction that mirrors the experience of others previously stigmatised. The nature of social interaction may define and redefine relationships until one succumbs and adopts an identity that fits in with how one previously treated those who have become one's peers. Self-stigmatisation is an acknowledgement of a sense of failure, when one does not fit in any more. The stigma is of loss of face and a lowered self-esteem.

Situational elements of stigma

The situational aspect of stigma is illustrated in a famous quote from Norman Tebbit, made during the aftermath of urban riots in the summer of 1981. He responded to a suggestion that rioting was caused by unemployment by saying: 'I grew up in the 1930s with an unemployed father. He did not riot. He got on his bike and looked for work, and he went on looking until he found it.' (Tebbit, 1981) This comment is stigmatising of people who do not gain work because they do not choose to seek a move from their home area to look for employment. It reinforces the stigma of unemployment in association with the region where people live – it is situational because it is based on location. It denies the right of individuals to find work in their home area, suggesting that those who do not leave, and presumably their families, children and communities are somehow failures; people are not achieving because they do not have jobs. Clearly, this is a social injustice when employment is viewed as something to be sought at any social cost to the individual. The individual is blamed rather than the lack of opportunity within a particular area.

Barnes and Mercer (2003: 9) discuss the divide between 'able-bodied' and disabled people, which I have chosen to call 'situational stigma' to differentiate it from social and structural stigma. An example that is provided of situational stigma within a group activity is of it taking place within the 'norms' of teen society: a conforming individual establishes a particular 'identity type', but 'fears' being identified as different to others in the 'core' membership group. This fear fits Barnes and Mercer's view that disabled people are seen as 'unfortunate'. The teen group in my example is the place to belong but is stigmatising of the individual who does not fit in; this can be due to the group norm of not accepting difference. This may be explained by the 'geek' factor, when the individual faces the possibility of rejection unless adopting the norms of the group, and this form of stigma is situational when an individual cannot gain a place in the group to achieve peer approval. Situational stigma in this example is similar to social stigma, except in this case the stigma is rejecting at the individual level of experience, where membership of a group is questioned; it is like a rejection from an exclusive club because of a failure to meet the membership criteria. This is unlike and indeed is the opposite of social stigma, where the identification with the group carries with it the stigma of a 'spoiled identity' (Goffman, 1963).

It should be clear that situational stigma has broader and narrower interpretations. At the broadest level whole communities are viewed as underachieving or are stereotyped as those from the 'bad estate'. At the individual level it is about rejection from possible social group membership and situational stigma is located between the social (an interactive form of stigma impacting on group identity) and structural (an official form of stigmatisation against individuals). In reality elements of each may overlap, although one may typify an experience better than another.

Structural aspects of stigma
The third form of stigma is structural, where, for example a condition or diagnosis may exclude opportunities. Gillman (2004: 253) cites the diagnosis of 'learning difficulty' that serves to promote 'prejudicial and discriminatory attitudes in some professionals, which may lead to disrespectful or dehumanising treatment of individuals who are seeking support'. She goes on to suggest that, once such a diagnosis is made, further conditions are sought to provide a resulting 'dual diagnosis'. In a sense the seeking for additional conditions is associative, in the belief that somehow one is a contagion of the other. 'Barriers to work for people with mental health problems include

structural factors, stigma and prejudice, attitudes and approaches of mental health services and the lack of well-run employment services' (Royal College of Psychiatrists, 2003: 3).

Stigma of a structural form can lead to oppressive practices. As Dominelli (1997) clarifies, racist attitudes may result from following embedded institutional practices that routinely discriminate against individuals from different races. It is in this sense that research by Burke (2005) indicated that young people with special needs had experienced exclusion from mainstream education. However, the research showed that the young people who were labelled as having 'special needs' later found a rewarding self-identity within a special group led and developed for such young people. The young people in this case experienced discrimination in a positive sense and having 'special needs' then became an activating device to improve the lots of the group so identified.

Models of disability

The prevalent models of disability seek to explain social experience which defines disability as a reactive condition due to the impact and effect of social interaction on individuals which transmute an impairment into an incapacity to engage with others: social experience constructs disability beyond the level of a specific impairment. The experience of socially constructed disability that results (i.e. the element of disability that induces reactions from others that serve to reinforce disability) is referred to as 'the social model of disability'. The social model suggests that disabled people are subject to oppression by non-disabled people (Shakespeare and Watson, 1998). This means that the disadvantage of disability arises from the unequal status that disabled people experience compared with non-disabled people. The example that illustrates this most simply is that of the wheelchair user who cannot access a building due to the steps that have to be negotiated; an experience encountered by Burke (2004: 129). In such a situation, the steps reinforce an individual's identity as disabled, whereas ramped access would not. The issue also links to the way individuals interact in everyday life, where attitudes define disability through the process of stigmatisation discussed earlier.

The sense of being different that is generated due to the social identity of disability is important to understand because a disabled identity often results from the expressive perceptions and actions of others and the label of disability is put onto individuals who might otherwise not consider themselves disabled or different. Some may wish to be identified as different, which is their right, but difference which is imposed by another is potentially discriminating no matter how well intentioned. It is part of normal interaction to express views – 'You say that because you are just...being smart' – but any extreme expression has the potential to become offensive – 'You say that because you are...disabled, black, and a woman.' In the social setting attitudes should promote acceptance of a person whether disabled or not – indeed, whether different or not – and in a physical sense too, barriers or obstacles that promote a sense of disability or discrimination should not be put in place. However, the fact that disabled people still encounter obstacles of both a social and physical kind means that barriers to disability remain part of daily activity.

In understanding the relationship of siblings to a brother or sister with disabilities the sense is that the 'disabling element' of the social model essentially identifies environmental exclusion as resulting from limited physical access for disabled people and which requires non-disabled people to perceive such restrictions as not being the fault of the disabled person. However, the realities are that disabled people feel blamed and ridiculed for their disability (Morris, 1996): the need is to challenge such views. Indeed, Thompson's (2001) model of anti-discriminatory practice is about changing individual, situational and cultural attitudes: these might equally apply to the social model of disability.

It is evident that disability (as a social construction) has become identified as a personal problem or condition that should be overcome on an individual basis: in turn this leads to social exclusion. The experiences of childhood disability become the property of the family as each member shares the experience of the others to some degree. In a perfect situation, where exclusion and neglect do not occur, this model of disability would cease to exist because it would not help an understanding of the experience faced by the 'disabled family as a unit. The need, therefore, is to examine the impact of stigma on specific groups of individuals and shows how stigma becomes an associative state for others who are close to such individuals, whether family members or professionals working with the family.

Disability by association

The concept of disability by association is built on the experience of siblings of disabled children (Burke, 2004). The sense of difference which disability imparts on siblings is partly explained by Wolfensberger (1998: 104) with reference to devalued people who, due to a process referred to as 'image association', are portrayed in a negative way. This happens when disabled people are stereotyped as some kind of 'evil villain': the image of Frankenstein, with a lumbering, awkward gait, a monstrous build, inarticulate speech and an apparent ability to murder. The image is of horror, the association of murderous intent with disability is a bad thing – almost a Pavlovian form in the classical conditioning sense, whereby disabled people must by association also be bad.

Unfortunately, the sense of 'image association' in a negative sense will often pervade the whole family and however they accommodate negative perceptions, such experiences are not restricted to those with disabilities themselves. Devaluing experiences are common to other disadvantaged groups. Indeed, Phillips (1998: 162) indicates 'children who are disabled, black, adopted or fostered can be stigmatised and labelled because they are different'. Disability is one area of possible disadvantage; race, class and gender are others, none of which I would wish to diminish by concentrating on disability. But disability in children becomes a family experience, and one that has a particular impact on siblings.

Disability is viewed as family matter when one child or, indeed, one member of the family might be described as disabled. In the experience of siblings I have shown that parents dealing with a disabled child's care needs find they have less time to devote to their non-disabled children, amounting to a form of neglect even though this might be inadvertent. The experience of siblings at school might reinforce a sense of being different because they can be identified with their disabled sibling; this I have represented in Figure 1.2 (from Burke, 2004) which shows the double impact of school and home life creating an identity of difference (to their peers) for the siblings of disabled children. It is as though the non-disabled children, as part of their upbringing, identify themselves as carrying part of the family's sense of being disabled. Non-disabled children, it appears, carry an invisible identity as a disabled child through the associative disability of their sibling.

The expectation for all children is that they should be cared for and experience some form of family life. The situation of siblings is that the experience and interaction with a brother or sister is for life unless some unfortunate circumstance interrupts that. Brothers and sisters will often have the longest relationship in their lives, from birth to death. It is partly because of this special relationship that, in my research bid to the Children's Research Fund, I was keen to explore the situation of siblings of disabled children.

The model represented in Figure 1.2 represents the process of disability by association reflecting the experience of neglect which siblings may face at home due to the competing and overwhelming needs of a disabled sibling, which may then be compounded by experiences of social exclusion that exist away from home. The latter may result from being picked on at school or from friends asking awkward questions about being a sibling of a disabled child, or from any number of social occasions that by themselves might seem innocuous, but in combination develop a sense of disability within the non-disabled sibling: becoming disabled by association.

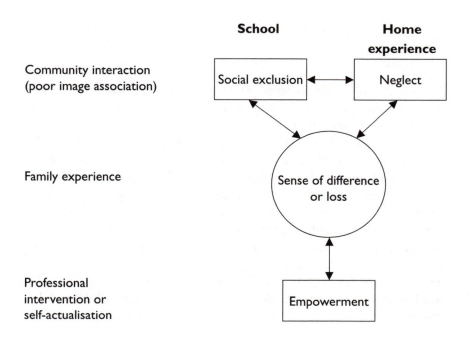

Figure 1.2 Disability by association (Source: Burke, 2004: 26)

Living with disability may make a family feel isolated and alone, especially if social encounters reinforce the view that a disabled person is someone who is not worthy. Another family may acknowledge differences as a welcome challenge, confirming individuality and a sense of being special, but the obstacles to overcome may be considerable.

Parents commonly understand the needs of siblings as siblings compete for their share of parental attention. Older siblings may share in the tasks of looking after a younger sibling. The brothers or sisters of disabled children, as demonstrated by my research (Burke and Montgomery, 2003), will usually help with looking after the disabled child. In gaining this experience, siblings are different to 'ordinary' siblings. Indeed, parental expectations may increase the degree of care that is required and any age disparity is removed, such that a younger child may help care for an older brother.

An example drawn from an interview with a parent of a disabled child helps to illustrate how avoidance may be construed as exclusion:

> I was walking along my home street pushing my young son in his buggy when I saw a near neighbour, with whom I'd always been on friendly terms, but had not seen for about six months. She crossed the road, to the wrong side for access to her home, avoided our possible encounter, only to

re-cross the road once we had passed each other. In my mind I debated the reasons for avoidance but found no happy solution! (Parent of a disabled child)

The question of avoidance arose because six months previously the child in question would play with the neighbour's child – both were of a similar age. It transpired that they had exchanged 'Thomas the Tank Engine' videos and had met at nursery. However, in the earlier period the child in the buggy had been 'normal'; since then he had become disabled, and when the incident above was experienced, the child was quadriplegic, sitting poorly in his chair and looking very different to the child the neighbour previously knew. The neighbour probably could not deal with all of this. Like many barriers faced by disabled families, the experience of simple avoidance was the beginning of an understanding of 'disability' as potentially excluding. This kind of experience engendered, for this parent, feelings of not belonging to the same group that existed before the child's debilitating illness. This was like joining an exclusive club as a parent of a disabled child, membership of which is imposed, not selected, and which then results in an invisible barrier between certain families and groups.

The sense is that 'normal' people are viewed as different and that leads to a stigma of association with disability. Disability, as expressed by Thomas (1999: 124) is a relationship between the powerless (those with an impairment) and the powerful (those without an impairment). Normality is about a lack of impairment and an impairment through the process of social interaction becomes a disability. When a person is stigmatised as disabled 'normal' people erect a barrier to exclude the 'infectiousness' of the perceived stigma. This means that associating with disability is likely to be transmitted to the normal world, and as such, it is feared. The impact of this is probably a result of negatively conveyed social attitudes. The escape route from the perception of disadvantage, or disability by association, is through some means of empowerment: that is, gaining a positive identity in relationships with others.

The application of associative disadvantage
In this introductory chapter, the intention has been to demonstrate that social disadvantage is a process that is transmitted, confirmed and attributed to certain groups of individuals, particularly, given my research, those with disabilities and those associated with disabilities. The model discussed suggests that disadvantage leads to social exclusion via a process of stigmatisation through social, structural and situational factors which construct both physical and attitudinal barriers for disabled individuals and for others

who might be identified as disadvantaged. Unfortunately, the power of negative identities is such that associative conditions also prevail and will include siblings, family members and those working in the field who deal with disadvantaged individuals. However, all is not gloom and negativity, with the lot of those that have being to denigrate and look down on those who have not. There is a glimmer of hope, and disadvantage and stigmatisation can turn into positive experiences, as my research with special needs children has demonstrated (Burke, 2005).

The model proposed is indicative that, despite positive developments, the social fabric of society in Britain is such that stigma remains a reality. It is because of this reality that the need exists for a model that has transferability across the spectrum of social need, which is often the manifestation of disadvantage and social exclusion. Consequently, this book takes a journey, in part it must be said, to address the stigma of disadvantage through associative conditions. The beginning is in extending the research into disability by association before considering how associative stigmatisation occurs within other service user groups, and within professionals working with such groups. The following chapters attest to the existence of stigma through association and the need to inform practice of its significance.

References

Abercrombie, N., Hill, S. and Turner. B.S. (2000) *The Penguin Dictionary of Sociology*. 4th edition. London: Penguin.

Banks, J.A. (1991) *Teaching Strategies for Ethnic Studies*. Needham Heights, MA: Allyn and Bacon.

Barnes, C. and Mercer, G. (2003) *Disability*. Cambridge: Polity Press.

Blackwell, D.L., Hayward, M.D. and Crimmins, E.M. (2001) 'Does childhood health affect chronic morbidity in later life?' *Social Science and Medicine 52*, 1269–84.

Bowlby, J. (1971) *Attachment and Loss. Volume 1: Attachment*. London: Penguin.

Burke, P. (2004) *Brothers and Sisters of Disabled Children*. London: Jessica Kingsley Publishers.

Burke, P. (2005) 'Listening to young people with special needs: the influence of group activities.' *Journal of Intellectual Disabilities 9*, 4, 359–76.

Burke, P. and Montgomery, S. (2003) *Finding a Voice: Expanding Horizons in Social Work and Allied Profession*. Birmingham: Ventura Press.

Cheetham, J. (ed.) (1982) *Social Work and Ethnicity*. London: George Allen & Unwin.

Denham, A. and Garnett, M. (2002) 'From the "cycle of enrichment" to the "cycle of deprivation": Sir Keith Joseph, "problem families" and the transmission of disadvantage.' *Benefits 10*, 3, 193–8.

Department of Work and Pensions (2005) *Research Report No 286 into Multiple Disadvantaged Groups in European Social Fund Objective 3 in England*. Press release 1 October. Available at www.dwp.gov.uk/mediacentre/pressrelease/2995/oct/emp111005.asp (accessed 2005).

Dominelli, L. (1997) *Anti-Racist Social Work*. Basingstoke: Macmillan.

Eysenck, A.R. (1971) *Race, Intelligence and Education*. Aldershot: Temple Smith.

Gillman, M. (2004) 'Diagnosis and Assessment in the Lives of Disabled People: Creating Potentials/Limiting Possibilities?' In J. Swain, V. Finkelstein, S. French and N. Oliver (eds) *Disabling Barriers – Enabling Environments*. 2nd edition. London: Sage Publications/Open University, p.253.

Goffman, E. (1963) *Stigma, Notes on the Management of Spoilt Identity*. London: Penguin.

Goffman, E. (1974) *Frame Analysis: An Essay in the Organisation of Experience*. London: Penguin.

Graham, H. and Power, C. (2004) *Childhood Disadvantage and Adult Health: A Lifecourse Framework*. London: Health Development Agency website, www.hda.nhs.uk/evidence (accessed 2006).

Hogan, M.F. (2003) *Achieving the Promise: Transforming Mental Health Care in America*. President's New Freedom Commission on Mental Health, Maryland. www.mentalhealthcommission.gov/reports/FinalReport/FullReport.htm (accessed 2006).

Hunt, P. (ed.) (1966) *Stigma: The Experience of Disability*. London: Geoffrey Chapman.

Jenkins, S.P. and Schluter, C. (2002) *The Effect of Family Income During Childhood on Later-Life Attainment: Evidence from Germany*. Institute for Social and Economic Research, http://ideas.repec.org/p/iza/izadps/dp604.html (accessed August 2006).

Joseph, K. (1972) The Cycle of Deprivation. Speech at Conference of Pre-School Playgroups Association, 29 June.

Lee, G. and Loveridge, R. (1987) *The Manufacture of Disadvantage*. Milton Keynes: Open University Press.

McGhee, J. and Waterhouse, L. (2002) Family Support and the Scottish Children's Hearings System. *Child and Family Social Work 7*, 273–83.

Morris, J. (1996) *Encounters with Strangers*. London: The Women's Press.

Parker, R.A. (1971) *Planning for Deprived Children*. London: National Children's Home.

Phillips, R. (1998) 'Disabled Children in Permanent Substitute Families.' In C. Robinson and K. Stalker (eds) *Growing Up with Disability*. London: Jessica Kingsley Publishers.

Royal College of Psychiatrists (2003) *Employment for All: Assisting People with Health Problems and Disabilities into Work*. House of Commons Work and Pensions Inquiry, www.rcpsych.ac.uk (accessed August 2006).

Rutter, M. and Madge, C. (1976) *Cycles of Disadvantage*. London: Heinemann Educational Books.

Shakespeare, T. and Watson, N. (1998) 'Theoretical Perspectives on Research with Disabled Children.' In C. Robinson and K. Stalker (eds) (1998) *Growing Up with Disability*. London: Jessica Kingsley Publishers.

Tebbit, N. (1981) Norman Tebbit Biography. Available at www.fandmpublications.co.uk/pages/normantebbitbiography1.htm (accessed 2006).

Thomas, C. (1999) *Female Forms: Experiencing and Understanding Disability*. Buckingham: Open University Press.

Thompson, N. (2001) *Anti-Discriminatory Practice*. 3rd edition. Basingstoke: Macmillan.

Toh, P. (2004) *Personal Experiences, HIV and Self-Stigma, Summary of Stigma Aids eForum discussion*. HDN, www.hdnet.org

Wolfensberger, W. (1998) *A Brief Introduction to Social Role Valorization: A High-Order Concept for Addressing the Plight of Socially Devalued People, and for Structuring Human Services*. 3rd edition. New York: Syracuse University.

Yang, H. and McMullen, M.B. (2003) 'Understanding the relationships among American primary-grade teachers and Korean mothers: the role of communication and cultural sensitivity in the linguistically diverse classroom.' *Early Childhood Research and Practice 5*, 1, http://ecrp.uiuc.edu/v5n1/yang.html (accessed August 2006).

Chapter 2

Looked After Children, their Parents, Disadvantage and Stigma

Catherine Deverell

The primary focus of this chapter is on children and young people who are looked after in public care and the disadvantage and stigma that they experience. The second part of the chapter considers the experience of the parents of these children, and there it is argued that they too are stigmatised and disadvantaged. The chapter ends with a discussion of some of the implications of these issues for social work practice.

The term 'disadvantage' is used to mean social exclusion or negative impact on life chances (as defined in Chapter 1) and stigma is identified as an undesirable difference in a person's identity as perceived by others (Goffman, 1963). It is worth noting that although the concepts of disadvantage and stigma are particularly relevant to looked after children and their parents *as a group*, they are a diverse group of individuals and some of the different experiences within it will be considered. Perhaps the most obvious distinction to be made is the legal basis on which a child is looked after.

The number of looked after children in England in March 2004 was over 61,000, an increase of 26 per cent over the previous ten years. Of that number approximately two thirds were subject to care and interim care orders (Sections 31 and 38 of the Children Act 1989) and around a third were accommodated on a voluntary basis (Section 20 of the Children Act 1989). A small additional number were looked after on the basis of compulsory orders such as Emergency Protection Orders (Section 44 of the Children Act 1989) (DfES, 2005).

The term 'looked after child' is used to refer to *all* those children who are placed by local authorities in foster care, residential care or with family and friends, whether the legal basis is voluntary or compulsory. In cases where a child is looked after on a voluntary basis, 'accommodated' under Section 20 of the Children Act, it is usually a constructive arrangement intended to support families. Local authorities' obligations to support children in need and their families generally appears in Section 17 of the Act and the placing of Section 20 'accommodation' in this part reinforces its voluntary nature. When a child is accommodated in this way, parents (mothers and fathers if they already had it) retain sole parental responsibility. The plans for accommodation are likely to be short term and time limited. Though some day-to-day decisions may be delegated to the carers (either foster or residential) it is the parents who would agree to this and the parents who would remain the main decision-makers regarding their child.

In contrast to this arrangement, interim care orders and care orders (Sections 38 and 31 of the Children Act 1989) are made by a court when a child is deemed to be suffering or likely to suffer significant harm and the harm is attributable to 'the care given not being what it would be reasonable to expect a parent to give', or in a much smaller number of cases, the child being 'beyond parental control' (Children Act, 1989). The local authority acquires parental responsibility. Parents do not lose their parental responsibility but the local authority has the power to determine the extent to which they can exercise it.

Even in these cases, where the arrangements for care are compulsory and the local authority has the power to make important decisions about the child, there remains, in the Act, an expectation of a continued role for parents unless it is not consistent with the welfare of the child. Whether the child is accommodated on a voluntary basis or in care under a legal order the local authority has a legal obligation to consult with the parents before any decision about their child is made (Section 22(4) of the Children Act 1989). There is also a presumption of contact with parents unless that would be contrary to the welfare of the child. Along with the principle that the child's welfare is of paramount importance, the principle of partnership with parents is one of the key messages of the Act.

Disadvantage, stigma and looked after children

Looked after children are disadvantaged on a number of fronts: before, during and after being looked after. They are disadvantaged by their pre-care experiences. Looked after children tend to come from the poorest families (Bebbington and Miles, 1989); more than 60 per cent have experienced abuse or neglect (DfES, 2005) and all have experienced the trauma of separation. Lack of planning for permanence (Rowe and Lambert, 1973), lack of placement stability (Berridge, 2000) and a lack of adequate focus on the education of looked after children (Jackson, 2001) have been identified as some aspects of 'care' itself being responsible for the failure to provide 'compensatory parenting' (Wade, 2003). Since the 1990s, when systematic measurements of the 'outcomes' for looked after children began to be made, there has been a growing awareness of the disadvantage that young people face at the other end of the care system: when they leave. A picture has emerged of young lives blighted by poor educational achievement, poor job prospects, teenage pregnancy, homelessness and youth crime (Social Exclusion Unit, 2003). There is therefore a complex combination of factors that contribute to the disadvantage experienced by looked after children. An overview of some of these factors and the stigma associated with the care system follows.

Pre-care experiences
Child abuse and neglect are the reasons for at least 60 per cent of the looked after children coming into care. They represent a very individual form of oppression often perpetrated by those closest to the child. The implications for looked after children who have been abused may be far reaching. There may be physical or psychological consequences leaving children with complex needs and behaviour that is difficult for carers to manage. The child may not have had the opportunity to form positive attachments, leading to difficulties in forming new relationships and in trusting people (Howe, 1995). These factors can damage the child's resilience and hamper their ability to face subsequent challenges (Daniel, Wassel and Gilligan, 1999).

Of the remaining 40 per cent of children, the main reasons for being looked after include 'absent parenting', 'family dysfunction', 'parent's illness or disability' and 'family in acute distress' (DfES, 2005). These reasons may not be as damaging as abuse and neglect and may necessitate short-term accommodation of the child rather than long-term care, but for many they represent a period of stressful and fraught family relationships and undoubtedly lead to some disruption for the child. In addition to this, the physical move from the family home to a foster home or residential care involves separation and loss (Fahlberg, 1994) not only from family members but also from the family home and familiar routines.

Children who are looked after are often already disadvantaged by a background of poverty. There does seem to be a correlation between children becoming looked after and socioeconomic disadvantage (Bebbington and Miles, 1989; Becker, 1997). Freeman and Lockhart in 1994 suggested, on the basis of their research in Strathclyde, that 78 per cent of children entering the looked after system originated from families in receipt of benefits (in Becker, 1997: 111). In their research review Aldgate and Statham (2001) found that families of children subject to care proceedings tended to have entrenched and longstanding multiple problems such as domestic violence, inadequate housing, living in poor neighbourhoods, suffering from poor health and misusing drugs and alcohol. Being poor in itself is likely to lead to a family being socially excluded, discriminated against and stigmatised (Thomas, 2005a) and the association of additional factors within the family such as these are likely to exacerbate those effects.

Disabled children and ethnic minority children (particularly those from Caribbean and mixed parentage backgrounds) are also over-represented in the looked after population. (Barn, Andrew and Mantovani, 2005; DfES, 2005a) For these groups the experience of exposure to disablism or racism may combine with and compound the disadvantage and stigma of being a looked after child.

Being in care

In his influential work on stigma, Goffman refers to 'an attribute that is deeply discrediting' (Goffman, 1963: 6) that makes a person different in a less desirable way from others. This undesirable difference leads to a 'spoiled identity' for the person. For looked after children, being identifiably 'different' is part of life. Children looked after in foster families are likely to be familiar with a different family culture from that within the foster family: 'customs about television, what happens at weekends, the use of space, in jokes, implicit and explicit rules...' (Sinclair, Wilson and Gibbs, 2001: 20). There are other factors visible to those outside the family. Examples include having a different surname to your carers, being from a different ethnic or religious background and living in a residential children's home rather than a family home, which could all set the child apart from his or her peers.

The involvement of social workers in itself may mark a child out as being different. Social workers operate within the framework of the Looking After Children system, a comprehensive system of assessment, planning, monitoring and reviewing of children's lives. This was developed in the early 1990s at a time of growing awareness and concern about the very poor outcomes for looked after children and of children 'drifting' in care without any proper care plans (Parker *et al.*, 1991). This level of intervention is comprehensive for good reason: it attempts to address these past failings of the care system. Despite this, a side effect of its very comprehensiveness may be to identify those children as different. The Looking After

Children system applies to all looked after children, those children volun-tarily accommodated as well as those looked after on the basis of legal orders. The 'corporate parent' is very obviously different from an ordinary parent. Regular review meetings, personal education plan meetings, regular visits from the social worker and contact arrangements with the family are just some of the commitments for the looked after child which are not a feature of the lives of most children and which may serve to identify that child as different.

Not just the social work process but *how* it is undertaken is also likely to impact on the sense of 'difference' felt by the child. One of the criticisms of the Looking After Children system is that the tick box format of some of the paperwork (Assessment and Action Records) introduces considerable bureaucracy into the relationship between the social worker and the child: that 'the completion of the booklets is likely to reinforce the sense of stigma and "abnormality" a young person might already feel whilst being "looked after"' (Garrett, 2003: 28). One answer to this criticism is that this paper-work is a 'tool' or a guide to the important areas that need to be addressed with the child if his or her developmental needs are to be properly assessed, which should not be mechanistically applied but should encourage the social worker to spend time with the child and engage in meaningful dialogue (Jackson, 1998).

One of the important roles of the 'corporate parent' is to protect vulner-able looked after children from harm. But the way in which this has been done in the past has sometimes served to identify these children as different. An example of this often identified by children is having to request special permission to sleep over at a friend's house (Munro, 2001; Thomas, 2005b). Most parents do not conduct Criminal Records Bureau checks (police checks) before agreeing to a sleepover. It seems that this concern of looked after children has been heard and has filtered down to practice that is more sensitive to children's needs to be treated in a similar way to their peers. More local authorities now delegate this sort of decision to carers (Thomas, 2005b).

The balance to be gained is, on the one hand, to have a level of interven-tion by the 'corporate parent' that is comprehensive enough to not only replicate the activities of a 'reasonable parent' but to compensate for the past harm, disruption and vulnerabilities of looked after children; and, on the other, to minimise the identification of those children as 'different'. Research by Sinclair *et al.* in 2001 ascertained that what looked after children wanted most of all was to be 'ordinary'.

There is much that social workers can do to address some of these diffi-culties in the way that they work with looked after children (Bell, 2002;

Bilton, 2003; Munro, 2001; Sinclair and Grimshaw, 1997). Some of these issues will be addressed in the last part of the chapter, where it is argued that the social worker can work within the Looking After Children system in a way that is child-centred, respectful of the individual child and sensitive to the child's need to be 'ordinary'.

Goffman's conceptualisation of stigma involves not only being visibly different but also that that difference is discrediting or negative. And there does seem to be a negative stereotyping of looked after children. Taylor (2003) identifies common perceptions that 'routinely link children in care with trouble…' arguably resulting in 'the discrimination and further stigmatisation of an already vulnerable population' (Taylor, 2003: 240). In fact only 6 per cent of looked after children are looked after because of their behaviour (DfES, 2005). One of the dangers of such negative perceptions of these children is that it creates an environment where they are more vulnerable to abuse because they are not taken seriously and any allegations that they make are less likely to be believed (Taylor, 2003). Although poor outcomes such as youth offending are associated with looked after children *as a group*, there is a danger that they may serve to taint the identity of *individual* looked after children and lower people's expectations about what they can achieve.

Instability and frequent changes of placement are recognised to be one of the most worrying shortcomings of the care system. In 2004, 13 per cent of all looked after children had moved placement at least three times in the previous year (DfES, 2005). Government policy has aimed to address this problem. The Quality Protects initiative, 1997–2005 (Department of Health, 1999), involved practice and policy changes and set targets to reduce the number of placement moves. Choice Protects, started in 2002 (DfES, 2003), is aimed at improving commissioning and provision of foster placements (Holland, Faulkner and Perez-del-Aguila, 2005). Though a fairly crude measure, government statistics indicate that there has been an improvement in placement stability for those in short-term placements (from 20% of looked after children moving three or more times a year in 2000 to 13% in 2004) although for those in longer-term placements the general improvement has not been as significant (still fewer than half the children who had been in care for four years had lived in the same placement for the last two years) (DfES, 2005). So, moving remains a feature of the lives of many looked after children. Even children placed 'long term' had experienced frequent moves before placement and most children in long-term foster care wanted to move less than they did (Sinclair, 2005). The importance of the continuity of affectionate relationships for a child's healthy emotional development is clearly established (Daniel *et al.*, 1999).

The trauma and loss experienced by children when they are separated from their primary attachment figures and from siblings, extended family, friends and neighbours is explained by Fahlberg (1994). And for some children this is an experience that is repeated several times, impacting on their ability to trust and affecting future relationships into adulthood (Daniel *et al.*, 1999). On a practical level too, there is a stigma involved in being the new child in the family, in school, and so on.

Placement moves often mean school moves and placement instability is linked with poor educational achievement (Jackson, 2001). Research consistently shows that the educational attainment of children and young people in care is much lower than that of the general population. In 2001–2002 only 8 per cent of year eleven pupils who had been in care for a year gained five or more GCSEs graded A*–C compared with 50 per cent of all young people (Social Exclusion Unit, 2003). A complex combination of pre-care experiences and the failure of the care system to adequately compensate for them contribute to the problem. Factors include previous abuse or neglect, untreated mental health problems, difficult behaviour contributing to a high rate of school exclusions, placement instability, low expectations of carers and teachers and insufficient importance being placed on education by social workers (Jackson, 2001; Martin and Jackson, 2002). Poor educational achievement has a negative impact on future life chances and is an important feature of the disadvantage that looked after children experience.

Leaving care
Poor educational attainment is just one of the ways in which looked after children are disadvantaged when they leave care. They are at higher risk of experiencing homelessness, unemployment, young parenthood and poverty (Stein, 2002). The transition into adulthood – a difficult time for many young people in normal circumstances – is likely to be more challenging still for those with the accumulated disadvantages of a history of care. Yet the age at which young people leave care is generally much lower (commonly 16 or 17 years) than their peers tend to leave home (commonly in their early twenties) (Hayden *et al.*, 1999). In addition to their young age, a lack of preparation for independence and of support afterwards has meant that the transition to independence has in many cases been less gradual and less supported than it has been for their peers, leaving them particularly vulnerable (Hayden *et al.*, 1999).

For the 20 per cent of looked after children of minority ethnic origin, their needs for good substitute parenting are the same as those of the white looked after children but they may also need 'help to deal with racism and with issues of identity and racial pride' (Thoburn, Norford and Rashid, 2000: 208). It may seem logical to suppose that because young people from ethnic minority groups are disadvantaged in terms of their educational and employment opportunities (Barn *et al.*, 2005; Social Exclusion Unit, 2003) that the disadvantage would be multiplied by their being in care, but the picture is more complex than that. Recent research by Barn *et al.* (2005) indicates that white, Caribbean and young people of mixed parentage fare worse in terms of educational attainment, placement disruption, homelessness and risky behaviour; whereas African or Asian young people did better educationally and experienced less placement instability than the other groups. The authors attribute this difference to the former group spending longer periods in care and experiencing more placement and school disruption, and therefore being so disadvantaged over such a period of time that by the time they leave care 'the disadvantages prove to be so overwhelming and long term that this accumulation impacts on subsequent life chances' (Barn *et al.*, 2005: 76).

Young people leaving care or having left care are also disadvantaged by the negative perceptions of others about them. In a peer research project by West (1995), of the young people interviewed only 10 per cent thought that it would make no difference if people knew they had been in care. Typical responses of others were to label the person as a troublemaker, to be curious or to express sympathy (West, 1995).

As well as the accumulated disadvantage resulting from the combination of factors identified above, stigma may also continue into adult life. Two studies focusing on young parents who were or had been in care illustrate this. In the first by Rutman *et al.* (2002) conducted in Canada, social workers' attitudes to young mothers in and from care were examined. They found that there was a belief about the 'inevitability of "the cycle"; of children in care begetting children who ultimately came into care'. The authors conclude that young mothers from/in care are stigmatised and that this leads to 'systematic and often relentless scrutiny and surveillance' (Rutman *et al.*, 2002: 149, 158). The second, by Tyrer *et al.* (2005), based in the UK, addressed the experiences of young fathers leaving care and revealed a similarly depressing picture. Though the fathers in the study expressed the importance of fatherhood to them, in fact they tended to have 'poor or non-existent' relationships with their children. The authors, acknowledging the difficulty in identifying causal factors, attribute this in part to the men finding it hard to form trusting relationships due to troubled family relationships and frequent moves during their time in care; the accumulation of disadvantage associated with care. In addition some support services 'bought in' to a 'stereotype of young men as feckless and unconcerned with their children' (Tyrer *et al.*, 2005: 1119).

Despite this there may be some benefits for care-leavers becoming parents themselves, one of which may be the acquisition of the role of parent rather than care-leaver, leading to a non-care status (Hutson cited in Stein, 2002: 30).

In summary, the disadvantage experienced by looked after children is a complex combination of factors before, during and after being in care, one of which is the negative perception of others towards them.

Disadvantage, stigma and the parents of looked after children

When children are looked after in public care, their parents often continue to be involved. Whether the child is looked after as part of a short-term voluntary arrangement to support a child in need and his or her family or, at the other end of the care spectrum, in a long-term plan for permanence, the role of the parents is often vital in the success of that plan for the child. Most looked after children have some sort of contact with their parents (Cleaver, 2000) and many (though by no means all) return home to parents sooner or later (Sinclair, 2005). As well as being involved on a practical level, parents may also play a role in meeting their child's need for an understanding of their identity. This is not to say that the role of parents is always a positive one for looked after children. Around 60 per cent of these children are looked after because they have been abused or neglected (DfES, 2005); the actions of the parent may be the reason why the child is in care and their continued involvement may need to be minimal in order for the child to be able to 'move on' psychologically (Sinclair, 2005). Whatever the level of involvement – even if it is work to enable parents to come to terms with having no contact with their children – the parents remain significant and the development of a positive working relationship between the social worker and parents is more likely to enable both to work together to promote the welfare of the child involved. If the social worker can seek to gain an understanding of the experience of these parents then this partnership is more likely to be successful. In this part, the parents' experience in relation to disadvantage and stigma will be explored.

Many of the factors discussed above that contribute to the disadvantage and stigma experienced by looked after children also apply to their parents. They are from the same socioeconomic backgrounds and, if parents have continued involvement with their children, their lives will also include contact with social workers, review meetings and organised contact sessions. Beyond this, though, there is additional stigma attached to having a child in care.

Research by Colton *et al.* (1997) identifies the stigma attached to child welfare services as having its origins in the Poor Law and then the work of the Victorian philanthropists 'rescuing' children from idle, feckless and harmful parents. This sense of stigma has 'continued to cling to all parties involved' (Colton et al., 1997: 248). Of all child welfare services, it was found that the most negatively perceived by both users and providers were residential and foster care. For Colton et al. some of the factors associated with stigma are the degree to which services are 'voluntary, inclusive and give rise to a sense of respect, worth and control within the individual'. Services with these characteristics are less stigmatising than those with the opposite. Perhaps, then, the stigma is less for those parents whose child is looked after on a voluntary basis than for those whose children are removed from them as a result of legal proceedings? Indeed the intention of the Children Act 1989, by drawing a distinction between this voluntary arrangement and 'care' resulting from court proceedings, sought to reduce the stigma of the use of care as a temporary support to families as well as to assuage parents' fears that if they put their children in care, they would not get them back (Thomas, 2005a).

For parents of children subject to legal orders the level of intervention is not voluntary (unless parents agree to the making of such orders) and is more intrusive in that the power to exercise parental responsibility with regard to their child is limited. This represents a significant disempowering of a part of life that most parents take for granted. The court process too may have a negative impact on parents' sense of respect, worth and control. The exposure of every detail of the parents' lives and the evidencing of the ways that they have either not parented their children well enough or have harmed their children is a necessary part of the process of determining whether a child has suffered or is likely to suffer significant harm (Children Act 1989). For some parents this can obviously cause a deep and traumatic blow to probably already low self-esteem. During court proceedings parents are represented by a legal advocate, but when the legal proceedings are over and if orders have been granted, that representation ends. The position of the parents at this time is a relatively powerless one.

Although the Children Act 1989 differentiates clearly between those arrangements that are voluntary and those which are compulsory the Looking After Children system does not seem to be as sensitive. The term 'corporate parent' and the procedures that go with it apply whichever basis the child is looked after even if it is on a voluntary basis with sole parental responsibility remaining with the parents. Garrett criticises the 'corporate parent' construct for this inaccuracy and also because it 'might be perceived as marginalising, even disparaging a child or young person's *actual* parents with whom the local authority is supposed to be working in partnership' (Garrett, 2003: 21). Rather than the stigma being reduced for parents whose children are looked after on a voluntary basis as was perhaps one of the intentions of the Children Act 1989, it is probably more likely that the stigma of 'care' extends to both groups of parents – that parents whose children are accommodated because the family needs support rather than because the children are at risk of harm are tainted with the negative connotations of the latter. Whatever the route into the looked after system, both parents and providers in the Colton *et al.* research agreed that having a child looked after in foster or residential care would result in greater negativity on the part of others than any other social work intervention. Aldgate points out that 'Parents in these families are in danger of being labelled "irresponsible" or "inadequate", and most will feel stigmatised as failed parents' (Aldgate in Triseliotis, 1980: 24).

As well as gaining the discrediting association of having a child looked after, parents also lose some of the status that being a parent carries. In our society, being a parent carries with it positive connotations and therefore that status is an important part of most parents' identity. There are practical aspects to the loss of the role of providing care to one's children: missing out on the activities and social aspects of being a parent, such as taking children to school and providing for their practical needs – even if the parents struggle with this part of parenting. What do parents tell their friends? Do they have one explanation for public consumption and another for themselves? Finally, how does this affect relationships within the extended family? The ripples of stigma may extend and be felt by siblings who have lost a sister or brother, grandparents who have lost a grandchild, aunts and uncles who have lost a niece or nephew and so on. The associations are potentially as wide as the network that surrounds the child.

As well as coping with stigma, parents will almost certainly experience a range of feelings associated with loss: 'from sadness to relief, from shame to anger, from bitterness to thankfulness' (Jenkins and Norman, 1972: 97). Jenkins and Norman explored the process of filial separation – the term a reference to Bowlby's 'maternal deprivation' (Bowlby, 1969) – finding that parents experienced a range of feelings. Sinclair describes the mixed emotions that parents may feel when their children become looked after:

> there are likely to be mixed emotions, feelings of loss, a sense of failure, a worry about how the event can be presented at school or to the neighbours, a concern about how their child may do when away from them and about whether he or she will cease to love them or fail to return. (2005: 61)

Sinclair found that some of these worries though stronger in parents whose children were removed compulsorily were also present in parents whose children were to be looked after on a short-term basis (Sinclair, 2005).

We cannot make assumptions about what parents are feeling. Yet being sensitive to parents' experience and perspective can only help the social worker to work in 'partnership' with parents, whether the end result of that partnership is to promote good quality contact for the child or a return home, or the relinquishing of the child to permanent substitute carers.

Social work practice

Social workers are uniquely placed as the key worker for the looked after child – the 'human face' of corporate parenting (Utting in Bilton, 2003: i) – but also as the main point of contact with the child's parents. The chapter ends with a brief exploration of some of the elements of this difficult role.

Social work with looked after children takes place within the framework of government policy and under New Labour 'a plethora of initiatives' (Fawcett, Featherstone and Goddard, 2003) have been devoted to the improvement in outcomes of looked after children while they are in placement and when they leave for independence. As a group, they fit easily into the government's social investment strategy and the targeting of certain socially excluded groups for policy attention. New legislation includes the Children (Leaving Care) Act 2000 which aims to delay the discharge of young people from care and increase the preparation and support they receive. The 2004 Children Act increases the responsibility of local authorities to promote the education of looked after children by making it a duty. The Choice Protects (DfES, 2003) initiative aims to improve the supply quality of foster care. The Quality Protects (Department of Health, 1999) initiative set out a number of objectives with attached targets and performance indicators such as reducing the number of placement moves, increasing the educational achievement and promoting the participation of looked after children in decision-making. This recent government focus on looked after children and outcomes has raised awareness of the social exclusion that they face and has directed resources at tackling some longstanding problems. For example, given the low priority that the education of looked after children received in the past, what improvement there has been in more recent years is likely to be at least in part due to Quality Protects (Fawcett *et al.*, 2003) Figures show a slight improvement in educational attainment and improvements in short-term placement stability (DfES, 2005).

Though there are some improvements in outcomes, there have been calls for caution in their measurement and interpretation (Thomas, 2005a). The underlying message of the focus on outcomes is that we should strive for the same outcomes for looked after children as for everyone else; yet as Thomas points out, everyone else's outcomes are not the same. The more disadvantaged children in society have poorer outcomes than the more privileged. This raises the question of standards and what the care system should be trying to do. The originators of the Looking After Children system (Jackson, 1998; Parker *et al.*, 1991) noted this point and viewed the system (and the Children Act 1989) as an opportunity to move away from the legacy of the Poor Law principle of 'less eligibility'. This principle states that children in care should not have better opportunities and should not receive advantages over and above those of a similar background and living at home. So what standards should be set for looked after children? Should they be the same as the poorest families or should they be the same as middle class families? Jackson writes: 'all we can do is to provide *the best* conditions for growing up that we can' (Jackson, 1998: 48, emphasis added). It is unjustifiable to have lower expectations and set lower targets than those expected not just for the most deprived children, but for 'most children'. Yet the task of providing parenting that is good enough to compensate for the disadvantage already experienced by these children is considerable and this puts the social worker in a difficult position of being tasked with what may be a near-impossible job:

> If the expectation is that the care system will undo all the disadvantage that children and young people bring with them when they enter it, then it will need to be resourced to a much higher level than it currently is. (Thomas, 2005a: 183)

Other criticisms of the focus on outcomes in both Quality Protects and the Looking After Children system centre around the constraints it places on the social worker's opportunity to work creatively with children. According to Garrett (2003) the amount of form-filling in the Looking After Children system means that the social worker is more like a research assistant. Munro says that the focus on targets and the amount of time completing paperwork takes away from social workers opportunities to form meaningful relationships with the children and to work on the less easily quantifiable tasks such as working on emotional and behavioural problems (Munro, 2001).

Answers to this criticism are that the paperwork in the Looking After Children system provides a framework rather than forms to be mechanistically filled in (Jackson, 1998), and that there is plenty of scope for creative work with looked after children. There is more to the role of the social worker than form-filling.

Two studies that sought the views of children indicate that the social worker's role is very important to looked after children (Bell, 2002 and Munro, 2001). When it works well – when there is continuity of the same social worker, when the social worker is reliable, available and respects the confidentiality of the child – then the social worker is a strong ally. In the

Munro study many of the children were critical of their experiences when these things did not happen (Munro, 2001). To looked after children who are not in a settled placement, their relationship with the social worker may be one of the more enduring ones in their lives, seeing them through several placement changes. In such cases the social worker may function as a 'secondary attachment figure' providing therapeutic opportunities within the relationship that may effect change in the child and allow the child an environment in which he or she can express his or her wishes and feelings (Bell, 2002).

Listening to those wishes and feelings and acting on them may also enable the social worker to lessen the stigmatising effect of being looked after. For example, children in the Sinclair *et al.* study (2001: 24) said that their 'family or school was turned into a branch office of social services'. A social worker sensitive to the stigma that the child may be feeling could arrange review meetings away from these venues or give the child a choice about where he or she would like the review to be held.

Another important part of the role of the social worker is an organisational one and planning the placement is part of that. Placement with family and friends is increasingly being used (Broad 2001); and it can offer continuity of family culture and may be less alien than care by strangers and perhaps less stigmatising. It could also be argued that foster care is less stigmatising than residential care because it more closely resembles the family life that most children experience. However, other factors may outweigh that of stigma and for some young people who do not want to live in a family, residential care may be the first choice (Frost, Mills and Stein, 1999). Only by ascertaining the child's or young person's views will the social worker be able to be sensitive to the stigma experienced and be aware of the child's view of what sort of placement would be preferred. Again, though, the social worker is likely to be constrained by resource issues in that the shortage of placements mean that the choice is likely to be limited (DfES, 2003).

Given the disadvantage experienced by looked after children and young people there is a danger of seeing them in a passive role of 'victims' of their unfortunate circumstances. One of the most encouraging aspects of policy and practice with looked after children and young people in recent years is the attention given to their rights to involvement and participation. In terms of policy, the Quality Protects initiative contains a specific objective (objective eight) relating to children and young people's participation. Indications are that there have been improvements in this area. Research by Thomas (2005b) seeking the views of child care managers in 1997 and then again in 2004 found that there was a perceived improvement in the levels of participation by children in decisions such as who should be invited to their review meeting. The positive advantages for looked after children of participating in decision-making are numerous. Among them is the positive effect it is likely to have on self-esteem and the child's sense of self-efficacy: both factors linked to the enhancement of resilience (Daniel *et al.*, 1999). In this way the child or young person is likely to be better equipped to cope with future challenges. And the promotion of the rights of looked after children collectively may also serve to promote a more positive identity thus offsetting the negative effects of stigma.

Working with the parents is also part of the social worker's role and it is an aspect that has the potential to challenge the values of the individual social worker. As an advocate for the child the social worker is often only too aware of the harm that has been done to that child by a parent and yet must put any personal feelings on hold and promote parents' 'human dignity and worth' (one of the BASW Values: British Association of Social Workers, 2002). The social worker is in a powerful position in relation to the parent. In the most practical ways – for example, deciding whether or not the parent receives a copy of a school report – the actions of the social worker make a huge difference to the parent's experience of their child being in care. The balance of promoting the rights of parents whilst always prioritising the rights of the child is not always straightforward and how an individual social worker responds to this balancing act depends to some extent on their own values about the rights of parents. The term 'partnership' often used is therefore not straightforward given the unequal distribution of power (Beckett and Maynard, 2005) yet to strive towards it is not only a moral and legal requirement (as outlined in the Children Act 1989); there are also pragmatic reasons for doing so if the interests of the child are to be promoted. Factors identified by Aldgate and Statham (2001), contributing to 'partnership' between social workers and parents were keeping parents informed, being clear about expectations and parents' rights, understanding about what services are available to them and involving them in decision-making. Cleaver (2000) found that building parents' self-esteem early in the placement was associated with successful maintenance of contact and reunification of children. If the social worker seeks to gain an understanding of the parents' experience then this sort of work is probably more achievable.

With the rising number of looked after children the question of returning them home again is very pertinent and, given the high cost of long-term care, parents can represent a valuable resource. However, research raises concerns that when children do return to the care of their parents after a period of time in care, they do not always fare well (Cleaver, 2000). Sinclair *et al.* found that children who returned home after a long period of being looked after tended to show difficult behaviour, did not make improvements in their educational performance and were more likely to be re-abused than those who remained looked after (Sinclair *et al.*, 2004). Clearly, assessments of risk and of parents' abilities to meet the needs of returning children are vital before a child is returned home. Yet there is evidence to suggest that returns home are often unplanned (Biehal, 2005). Understanding how the parent will manage and support the child to manage the stigma of 'care' on the child's return may well need to be part of that assessment.

In addition to assessment, support is a major issue in the reunification of children from care. Skuse and Ward (2003) found that such support tends to be patchy and Sinclair (2005) identified a need for better support for parents after children are returned to them. Just as well-resourced family support services are important in preventing admission to care, they are perhaps even more vital on children's return home. The resources available to families are also an issue in a more general sense. Ward, Skuse and Munro (2005) found that one of the aspects of care that the children in their study appreciated was the material benefits of being in foster care compared to what they had experienced before care. This raises the question of what standard of living they should expect when they go home and leads back to the argument that it is important that structural inequalities and improving the outcomes of all disadvantaged children are addressed.

Conclusion

There is no doubt that looked after children experience disadvantage. This chapter has necessarily been as much an overview as an examination, purely because there are so many contributing factors. The factors contributing to disadvantage often exist before a child becomes looked after, the experience of care may fail to compensate or may even exacerbate existing problems and the accumulation of disadvantage by the time a young person leaves care is likely to impact on future life prospects. There has been considerable focus on looked after children in terms of policy and developing practice in the last decade with the aim of improving their outcomes. Although this focus is necessary if the complex needs of this group are to be met and the factors contributing to disadvantage addressed, to some extent it makes them more visible and may actually make being looked after more stigmatising. Despite this there is much that the social worker (as the key representative of the 'corporate parent') can do to address the stigmatising aspects of care. The promotion of children and young people's rights to participate in decision-making, for example, may promote a more positive identity for looked after children and therefore offset the stigma of being a child or young person in care.

Like their children, the parents of looked after children also experience disadvantage and stigma. They may be responsible for their child becoming looked after, yet there are clear reasons for social workers to work closely with them. They remain significant to their child, may remain involved in contact arrangements and may in the end provide the route out of the care system for their child.

References

Aldgate, J. and Statham, J. (2001) *The Children Act Now: Messages from Research.* London: The Stationery Office.

Barn, R., Andrew, L. and Mantovani, N. (2005) *Life after Care. The Experiences of Young People from Different Ethnic Groups.* London: Joseph Rowntree Foundation.

Bebbington, A. and Miles, J. (1989) 'The background of children who enter local authority care.' *British Journal of Social Work 19,* 5, 349–68.

Becker, S. (1997) *Responding to Poverty: The Politics of Cash and Care.* London: Longman.

Bell, M. (2002) 'Promoting children's rights through the use of relationship.' *Child and Family Social Work 7,* 1–11.

Berridge, D. (2000) *Placement Stability.* Quality Protects Research Briefing No. 2. London: Department of Health.

Biehal, N. (2005) *Reuniting Looked After Children with their Families: A Research Review.* York: JRF. Available at www.jrf.org.uk/knowledge/findings/socialpolicy/0056.asp (accessed February 2006).

Bilton, K. (2003) *Be My Social Worker: The Role of the Child's Social Worker.* Birmingham: British Association of Social Workers.

Bowlby, J. (1969) *Attachment and Loss, Volumes 1 and 2.* New York: Basic Books.

British Association of Social Workers (2002) *Code of Ethics for Social Work.* Birmingham: BASW.

Broad, B. (ed.) (2001) *Kinship Care. The Placement Choice for Children and Young People.* Lyme Regis: Russell House Publishing.

Cleaver, H. (2000) *Fostering Family Contact: A study of Children, Parents and Foster Carers.* London: The Stationery Office.

Colton, M., Drakeford, M., Roberts, S., Scholte, E., Casas, F. and Williams, M. (1997) 'Social workers, parents and stigma.' *Child and Family Social Work 2,* 247–57.

Daniel, B., Wassell, S. and Gilligan, R. (1999) *Child Development for Child Care and Protection Workers.* London: Jessica Kingsley Publishers.

Department of Health (1999) *The Government's Objectives for Children's Social Services.* London: The Stationery Office.

DfES (2003) *Every Child Matters.* London: The Stationery Office.

DfES (2005) *Children Looked After By Local Authorities Year Ending 31 March 2004. Volume One: Commentary and National Tables.* London: The Stationery Office.

Fahlberg, V. (1994) *A Child's Journey through Placement.* London: British Agencies for Adoption and Fostering.

Fawcett, B., Featherstone, B. and Goddard, J. (2003) *Contemporary Child Care Policy and Practice.* Basingstoke: Palgrave Macmillan.

Frost, N., Mills, S. and Stein, M. (1999) *Understanding Residential Child Care.* Brookfield, VT: Ashgate.

Garrett, P.M. (2003) *Remaking Social Work with Children and Families: A Critical Discussion on the 'Modernisation' of Social Care.* London: Routledge.

Goffman, E. (1963) *Stigma: Notes on the Management of Spoilt Identity.* London: Penguin.

Hayden, C., Goddard, J., Gorin, S. and Van Der Spek, N. (1999) *State Child Care: Looking After Children?* London: Jessica Kingsley Publishers.

Holland, S., Faulkner, A. and Perez-del-Aguila, B. (2005) 'Promoting stability and continuity of care for looked after children: a survey and critical review.' *Child and Family Social Work 10,* 29–41.

Howe, D. (1995) *Attachment Theory for Social Work Practice.* Basingstoke: Macmillan.

Jackson, S. (1998) 'Looking after children: a new approach or just an exercise in formfilling? A response to knight and caveny.' *British Journal of Social Work 28,* 45–56.

Jackson, S. (2001) *Nobody Ever Told us School Mattered: Raising the Educational Standards of Children in Care.* London: British Agencies for Adoption and Fostering.

Jenkins, S. and Norman, E. (1972) *Filial Deprivation and Foster Care.* New York and London: Columbia University Press.

Martin, P.Y. and Jackson, S. (2002) 'Educational success for children in public care: advice from high achievers.' *Child and Family Social Work 7,* 121–30.

Munro, E. (2001) 'Empowering looked after children.' *Child and Family Social Work 6,* 2, 129–38.

Parker, R., Ward, H., Jackson, S., Aldgate, J. and Wedge, P. (1991) *Looking After Children: Assessing Outcomes in Child Care. The Report of an Independent Working Party Established by the Department of Health.* London: HMSO.

Rowe, J. and Lambert, L. (1973) *Children Who Wait: A Study of Children Needing Substitute Families.* London: Association of British Adoption Agencies.

Rutman, D., Strega, S., Callahan, M. and Dominelli, L. (2002) '"Undeserving" mothers? Practitioners' experiences working with young mothers in/from care.' *Child and Family Social Work 7,* 149–59.

Sinclair, I. (2005) *Fostering Now: Messages from Research.* London: Jessica Kingsley Publishers.

Sinclair, I., Baker, C., Wilson, K. and Gibbs, I. (2004) *Foster Children: Where They Go and How They Get On.* London: Jessica Kingsley Publishers.

Sinclair, I., Wilson, K. and Gibbs, I. (2001) '"A life more ordinary". What children want from foster placements.' *Adoption and Fostering 25,* 4, 17–26.

Sinclair, R. and Grimshaw, R. (1997) 'Partnership with parents in planning the care of their children.' *Children and Society 11,* 231–41.

Skuse, T. and Ward, H. (2003) *Listening to Children's Views of Care and Accommodation.* Report to the Department of Health. Loughborough: Centre for Child and Family Research, University of Loughborough.

Social Exclusion Unit (2003) *A Better Education for Children in Care.* London: SEU.

Stein, M. (2002) 'Young People Leaving Care: A Research Perspective.' In A.Wheal (ed.) *The RHP Companion to Leaving Care.* Lyme Regis: Russell House Publishing.

Taylor, C. (2003) 'Justice for looked after children.' *Probation Journal 50,* 3, 239–51.

Thoburn, J., Norford, L. and Rashid, S.P. (2000) *Permanent Family Placement for Children of Minority Ethnic Origin.* London: Jessica Kingsley Publishers.

Thomas, N. (2005a) *Social Work with Young People in Care.* Basingstoke: Palgrave Macmillan.

Thomas, N. (2005b) 'Has anything changed? Managers' views of looked after children's participation in 1997 and 2004.' *Adoption and Fostering 29,* 67–77.

Triseliotis, J. (1980) *New Developments in Foster Care and Adoption.* Henley-on-Thames: Routledge and Kegan Paul.

Tyrer, P., Chase, E., Warwick, I. and Aggleton, P. (2005) '"Dealing with it": experience of young fathers in and leaving care.' *British Journal of Social Work 35,* 1107–21.

Wade, J. (2003) *Leaving Care.* Quality Protects Research Briefing No. 6. London: Department of Health.

Ward, H., Skuse, T. and Munro, E.R. (2005) '"The best of times, the worst of times." Young people's views of care and accommodation.' *Adoption and Fostering 29,* 8–17.

West, A. (1995) *You're on Your Own: Young People's Research on Leaving Care.* London: Save the Children Fund.

Chapter 3

Childhood Disabilities and Disadvantage: Family Experiences

Peter Burke and Benedict Fell

This chapter applies the concept of disadvantage by association to families and explains how practitioners may improve their understanding of the impact of disability using an assessment framework.

The incidence of childhood disability, as identified by Burke (2004), affects about 250 families in an average health authority of 500,000 people (see Joseph Rowntree Foundation, 1999). In other words it is not uncommon. Within such an area research shows disabilities across a broad spectrum of conditions and while listing conditions does not explain their causation, or indeed, the impact on the individual, it will at least help the reader to think of disabilities not so much as a homogeneous group, but rather as representing diversity and change for those categorised as 'disabled'. We may also begin to ponder the impact of such conditions, the need to describe experiences generally and specifically. Accordingly, while presenting grouped data, it is also important to introduce the singularity of individual experiences; to reflect, in the form of representation, each person's reality.

This chapter reports data gathered as part of a follow-up study to that produced by Burke and Montgomery (2003) and Burke (2004). This new research involved 60 families; the earlier study included 56 families. In both studies, interviews with families and siblings featured. An explanation of the methodology follows although more detail on how the research design evolved is provided in the original research in Burke (2004) and a discussion of a number of associated ethical issues involved in interviewing families is clarified in Burke (2005).

Hypothesis testing

It was hypothesised that the nature of disability by association may change over time and was, therefore, not 'fixed' by one typical response as appeared to be indicated in the earlier research of Burke and Cigno (1996) and Burke (2004). In part, this would fit a bereavement model of reactions (e.g. Kübler Ross, 1969) or a transitional adjustment to disability (e.g. Hopson, 1981). However, the earlier research suggested that adjustments to disability in the family were not necessarily sequential, as in a staging reaction, but appeared to plateau at a particular reaction type; for example, an angry reaction due to continued difficulties in having 'needs' met. What was identified was an occasional experience of regression back to an earlier stage of reaction without particular recourse to ever achieving a stage beyond that of the plateau, which might be short of acceptance or accommodation of the diffi-culty or difference perceived by the family. This further study should clarify the nature of such reactions, given that such reactions are not necessarily linear, or sequential, but might be subject to change over time.

Methods

This follow-up study was initiated for two main reasons:

1. to act as a reliability test on the earlier research

2. to clarify, whether 'disability by association', which had been identified by 'typical' response sets in the earlier research, had greater dimensionality.

The new study utilised a survey questionnaire approved by the University of Hull's Ethics Committee within the Faculty of Health and Social Care, with funding provided by the Higher Education Funding Council for England (HEFCE) and followed research allocations to the university. In order to progress with the research both researchers were subject to clearance through the Criminal Records Bureau (CRB) system to ensure that children were not at any risk in the interview stages of the research.

The questionnaire used in the study was the same as that reported by Burke (2004), which had been piloted and which is discussed in detail in Burke and Montgomery (2001). A similar research instrument for the main survey, in a related study, is about children with special needs, and is reported in Burke (2005). As researchers we had confidence that the instru-ment worked and using a questionnaire that was basically similar to those used before meant variables for analysis could be readily identified. Conse-quently, we had a tried-and-tested survey research instrument that categorised coded variables for examination by the Statistical Package for the Social

Sciences (SPSS). This produced frequency tables for descriptive information. This quantitative data were complemented by qualitative information generated through follow-up interviews with a sample of family interviews and, with permission, further interviews with the siblings of the non-disabled children. This helped capture what Greene and Hill (2005: 4) refer to as the 'richness of children's lives'.

The study was conducted in two stages. The first stage involved a questionnaire sent to 499 addresses via three different routes. The second stage involved interviews with families and siblings of non-disabled children. Previous work (Burke, 2004; Burke and Cigno, 1996, 2000) had focused on disabled children, and consequently we had established contacts with interested organisations in the north of England. Contacts included siblings groups in Merseyside, north Lincolnshire and East Yorkshire. Eighty invitation packs, including the questionnaire and letter of introduction, were sent on our behalf to parents of disabled children attending a special school in East Yorkshire. Twenty-five packs were distributed to addresses to a database in Merseyside. Finally, 394 questionnaires were distributed to addresses in north Lincolnshire. It was not possible to determine (primarily for confidentiality reasons) which of these families received the questionnaires distributed on our behalf – inevitably we were unable to verify whether in fact all the questionnaires were actually distributed and can only report on the numbers sent out.

We cannot say with complete confidence if distribution of the questionnaire reached the families that met the criteria of the research, i.e., families with a disabled child and other siblings. Out of 499 questionnaires, only 60 questionnaires were returned. This represents a very low and disappointing response rate of 12.2 per cent. However, given that this was a follow-up to the initial research, which had a response rate of 68 per cent, we were interested to see whether our analysis of the results would show any identifiable differences from the original study. The major difference to the earlier study was that the areas represented by the research were demographically more varied and representative of a broader-based catchment of respondents. If the findings from the earlier study were confirmed, then the confidence in the original research would be increased; if not, then the research might raise question for further areas of examination.

Interviews

Interviewing young children often demands skilful adaptation of the processes used with adult participants (Darlington and Scott, 2002). The need for confidentiality and the steps to ensure anonymity were explained in the introductory letter sent to families and to all participants at the time of the interview. All names used in direct quotes from participants/case studies are fictitious to preserve anonymity: this follows advice by Grinyer (2002) (see also Malin and Wilmot, 2000) that it is accepted practice not to identify research participants, although the view might be challenged if one participant endangered another.

Parental approval was required prior to interviews with young people, which in combination with approval from the young people (as indicated by Ramcharan and Cutcliffe, 2001) enabled the interviews to go ahead. Thus, the interviewers in this study (both qualified social workers) took care to explain the research in straightforward terms to the young people and to continually reiterate that the young person could, at any time during the process of interview, end further discussion; they could say 'Stop' or 'I don't want to go on', or just leave the room. Clearly, many of the issues that could have arisen in the course of interview could be unsettling or anxiety provoking.

In the earlier pilot study by Burke and Montgomery (2003) it was clear that younger siblings might not fully appreciate that their brother or sister was actually disabled, and we chose not to interview young people under the age of eight years for this reason – we did not wish to construct a notion of disability in the young person's mind. The evidence from Bridge (1999) suggested that children as young as four or five years were aware of their sibling's disability; however, we felt that some latitude should be given when it came to interview and so we chose an older age range for that purpose. We also followed our prior practice in that we considered children over the age of eight would have, in development terms, sufficient understanding of their home circumstance to offer their views, although, even in such circumstances, we remained mindful of any assumptions we might make concerning the siblings' actual interpretation of the meaning of disability.

The interviews were conducted in an informal open-ended manner (see Burke, 2005) to lessen anxiety. Where it became apparent that a child was 'stuck' or was becoming 'upset' attention was diverted to something less intense, for instance, hobbies, music or football. At the end of each interview, the interviewer took extra care to make sure the child was not leaving the interview in a distressed state and the children were thanked for their input. Interviews were mainly held in the family home, apart from a minority that were conducted over the telephone. In all, 15 young people participated in interviews; none requested that the interviews should end early.

Child disability and diagnosis

The incidence of disability identified in the research of Burke (2005), within an independent education advisory body covering an area similar to that of a health authority, indicated conditions such as learning difficulties, dyslexia, autism and dyspraxia. In an earlier study, on siblings of disabled children, disabilities were characterised by conditions such as Down's syndrome, cerebral palsy, microcephalia or even were simply identified as 'unknown' at the time of the investigation (Burke and Montgomery, 2003).

On the returned questionnaires in this study, parents indicated that their disabled children (N = 60) (N represents the total population) had a range of diagnosed conditions, many with more than one disability – these children were identified by the researchers as having 'multiple disabilities'. This combined category was the largest (n = 22, 36.7%) (n represents the proportion or percentage of the total population N) in the survey. Subsequent conditions were identified as on the autistic spectrum (n = 11, 18.3%), cerebral palsy (n = 5, 8.3%), epilepsy and Down's syndrome (for each, n = 4, 6.7%). Fewer than one in five parents (n = 11, 18.3%) were aware of their child's disability at birth.

Approximately two thirds of parents (n = 35, 66.3%) received a diagnosis after their child was ten months old, which compares with the earlier research of Burke and Montgomery (2003) where approximately half were diagnosed after the age of one year (n = 29, 51.2%). Both samples featured autism as a large proportion of the disabilities indicated and in both studies parents reported, with a degree of uncertainty and building suspicion, that their child (later diagnosed as autistic) had had some 'unknown condition' in early infancy.

It is evident that childhood disabilities may be identified at any time not necessarily at birth, sometimes at the prenatal stage, sometimes at birth and sometimes much later when the child attends school. Usually parents know that their child is 'different' in some way, but it is not necessarily so. The trouble is that disabilities are diverse, although few people have not encountered some form of disability, whether immediately recognisable or not.

Labels and transitions

It is evident from our work that parents who do not know that a child's condition has a medical label will nevertheless suspect their child is in some way different, and such parents persist in seeking a medical explanation for the differences perceived. Labels, however, serve only to identify a diagnosis of difficulty or difference; they do not explain who the child is, nor do they necessarily change family relationships, but inevitably a change takes place, and a long road to disability awareness will begin. The impact to the family may be, initially, as one parent said to one of us:

> like learning that your child has a disability is simply like a birthday, one day they are one age, the next day another and only one day has passed. Diagnosis is like that, only someone has put a label on your child, but the child is still the same child you knew before you were told.

For another parent, diagnosis was experienced as a 'double-edged' sword – it brought about 'peace of mind' but also a certain sense of guilt that the parent in question should have sought 'official recognition' sooner.

It is apparent that when parents see their child, their infant, they see the child they wanted. Perhaps some congenital conditions raise questions, but some conditions are invisible; in these latter cases there is no preconceived judgement and the infant, as one expects, is accepted. Unfortunately, the world is such that acceptance is not the only course, and sometimes parents, or one parent, may not accept their child. The issue of acceptance usually occurs before the child has an understanding of disability itself; the social stigma of disability is a situation that parents encounter from the early stage of diagnosis and understanding, and in many ways, their experience is of discrimination as though they themselves were in fact disabled. Disability by association suggests that the impact of living with disability is such that family members may feel they have an 'invisible' disability themselves. Part of this understanding of associative conditions involves transitional adjustments, accepting changes and getting on with life. Life is not, however, so simple, and transitional adjustments are fraught with uncertainty (see Burke and Cigno, 1996: 114).

In some ways, learning that a child is disabled later means that attachments are formed before a sense of disability has established itself. Learning at birth or before birth may be engaged with some sense of rejection once the realisation that the child is disabled is established. Labels do matter but when the attachment is strong they tend not to get in the way too much for the immediate family, but the social expectation on the child may not be so easy: while parents and siblings make adjustments, the world beyond the family may not be so accepting. The condition we refer to as 'disability by association' is about that divide between acceptance and rejection that forms part of the experience of many, but this is intricately bound up in the social experience of the child with disabilities and members of the family who experience disability by association.

When asked if the experience of having a disabled child was in any way 'different' to that of having a non-disabled child, this parent's response was typical:

> Caring for a disabled child has proved to be something more difficult and life changing than anything I could imagine. Everything generally takes longer, everything is different.

The impact of disabilities in families is clear, although it cannot and should not be assumed that this impact will be the same for all families. Each child is different, each experience of disability is different. Inevitably, the individual level of need – whether for a disabled child, reacting to the experience of his or her disability, or for the sibling and family of the disabled child – will vary to a considerable degree. The extent to which the family feels 'disabled' by association does indeed appear to have a full spectrum effect from the highly positive experience to those that are reported in a negative way. Our findings would support the earlier results from Burke (2004).

The experience of caring for a disabled child must also affect siblings, as the above indicates that more time and effort is required to help the disabled child manage daily needs whether with personal care or in terms of protection from possible dangers. This means that siblings will necessarily experience less attention within their family and one unintended consequence of living with disability is that their time is also taken up in assisting in the care of their disabled sibling.

The experience of childhood disability

In Burke (2004), the concept of disability by association is discussed. That study led to this text, which defines stigma by association in Chapter 1. Suffice to repeat, associative disadvantage results from the relative neglect siblings experience at home and the change in status experienced in social and educational settings. In Burke (2004), the reaction to such experiences is explained by considering the applicability of the stages of the Kübler Ross bereavement cycle to the case studies, and determining whether a positive or negative association is evident; this is considered to mirror to some degree the experience of being a sibling with a disabled brother or sister.

The case of John that follows shows how someone who is disabled experiences a secondary, additional form of disability; in this case, a physical disability is associated with a lowered expectation of academic achievement which is likely to reduce self-esteem and motivation. This also occurred in another case (Burke, 2005: 68) when Alan was told his school could do nothing for him, prior to his being enabled to achieving through the help provided within a group setting.

The case of John: A negative association with a disability

John, aged 14 years, attends a mainstream school. He uses a wheelchair and the school has provided ramps and a lift to access classrooms on the first floor, so John may join his peers in lessons. The school has a new sixth-form block; its first floor classrooms are not accessible to a wheelchair because the head teacher's view is: 'Well, if John manages to get to sixth form, we will install a lift.' The latter conveys the expectation that John is not intellectually gifted enough to gain the GCSEs needed and will only achieve at a level too low to warrant the expectation of future education at AS or A level. This is equivalent to saying to an able-bodied child: 'We will only put stairs to the first floor if you are clever enough to pass the exams.' In such circumstances, schools would be very busy if they only provided the necessary facilities for sixth-form entry after the exam results.

John has a severe physical impairment and cannot climb stairs. His academic performance is, nevertheless, average despite the difficulty he has in producing written work (aided by computer) and in focusing his attention when subject to physical tremors. His achievements, one would think, were considerable as he maintained academic achievements on par with his peers.

DISCUSSION

This above example is clearly reflecting a kind of disability by association; the association is that physical disability carries with it an intellectual impairment when the reality is that neither is automatically dependent on the other. The sense of disability by association has, in its enactment, an unequal project of expectation as experienced by John who attended a highly regarded secondary school.

It is not too difficult to imagine the frustration when a new sixth-form block was constructed at the school, without a lift to the first floor, at a time when John was beginning to achieve academic scores that would enable him to transfer to sixth form. The matter of not having a lift was discussed with the head teacher who responded by saying he would put in a lift on the condition that John succeed in gaining the academic requirements to enter sixth form. This sounds obliging enough, except it is the equivalent to saying to a non-disabled child, 'If you do well enough to get to sixth form, we will put in a staircase.' What this lacking of understanding shows is that everyday expectations for people without disabilities should be matched for people with disabilities; indeed, if this is followed through to its logical conclusion, the equalisation that is needed should include some additional mechanism such that disabled people are not disadvantaged.

John has had a barrier imposed that illustrates a form of structural stigma, as its imposition is due to the attitudes of those in authority. This impacts on his already difficult learning experience, almost like making a qualification practically unobtainable, as if the school is saying: 'Sorry you have no chance of getting to sixth form, so we will not even consider putting a lift in for you.' The same obstacle is also a barrier to any other child with mobility problems should they ever attend the school. The associative element of disability for the child with disabilities is simply this: 'You are physically disabled therefore you are not expected to achieve academically.' Disability by association places one element of disability onto every other potential channel of achievement – if you cannot do this, then you cannot do anything else either. Such an approach is little more than a stereotyping of an individual and this type of situational disadvantage amounts to oppressive practice.

Advantage and disadvantage

The majority of respondents in our survey (n = 49, 81%) felt that their non-disabled children had benefited by having a disabled brother or sister. Most responses surrounding the nature of this 'benefit' centred on the attributes that non-disabled siblings had developed as a direct consequence of their disabled sibling. These included increased tolerance of 'difference' and challenging behaviour; a greater empathy and understanding of disabled people and an improved caring attitude to others.

> It has made Joanne [non-disabled sibling] more accepting of people with disabilities and she's not fazed or frightened. She's developed a caring nature and wants to be a nurse. (Joanne's mother)

> My children have qualities lots of kids don't possess. They are aware of disability, never judge other children's behaviour and appear mature, compassionate, tolerant and caring in general. They also have natural defence mechanism towards disabled people, especially their own brother and sister. (Mother)

> It has made her [non-disabled sibling] more accepting that everyone is different. (Father)

> Michael [non-disabled sibling] now understands that everyone is different. He also can use his own judgement on people. He realises life is not a bed of roses and you have to work at what you want to achieve. (Father)

Conversely, a further finding from the survey data was the number of parents (n = 51, 86.4%) who felt that their non-disabled child had also been disadvantaged by having a disabled sibling (see Table 3.1). It is a complex equation which identifies that living with disability disadvantages children; yet at the same time it confers the positive benefits of acceptance and maturity. It is helpful to explore, however, the make-up of the apparent disadvantaging experience.

The nature of the disadvantage mentioned in Table 3.1 included two areas that received the most frequent responses. These are represented in Table 3.2 as restricted social activities (n = 28, 56%) and which might link to a sense of social stigma if these impacted on the child's peer group, and less attention from parents (n = 12, 24%) which equates with form of situational stigma (see Chapter 1) if construed as unavoidable neglect.

Table 3.1 Perceived disadvantage

	Frequency	%
Yes	51	86.4
No	8	13.6
Total	59	100.0

Table 3.2 Type of disadvantage

	Frequency	%
Restricted activities	28	56.0
Less attention from parents	12	24.0
Picked on at school	3	6.0
Noisy/disturbed	3	6.0
Additional responsibilities	3	3.0
Looked after by others	1	2.0
Total	50	100.0

Having restricted activities – that is, non-disabled children being able to do less from the limitations arising because of living with a disabled child – was the most reported response. Parents indicated that activities sometimes had to be cut short because of a disabled child's distress or challenging behaviour. In other cases, the sheer effort and time needed to prepare a disabled child to go out meant that it was often preferable not to bother with the activity, and this led to an increasing reluctance to pursue further activities. In addition, if a parent was alone or his or her partner was at work and the disabled child had to be looked after at home, the lone parent could not accompany non-disabled children to their activities and this had an impact on them. A more general response was parental awareness that their non-disabled child received less attention because of the time and energy needed to attend to their disabled child, as reflected in Table 3.1, meaning that their non-disabled child experienced a sense of neglect in the home.

In contrast with this lack of or reduced parental attention, it is evident from Table 3.3 that 77.4 per cent (n = 45) of the non-disabled children were involved in caring for their disabled sibling; in other words more than three quarters of siblings helped look after their disabled brother or sister. This compares favourably with the earlier figure reported by Burke (2004) where 82 per cent (n = 56) of parents reported that siblings helped with the care of their non-disabled siblings.

Table 3.3 Siblings caring for disabled brothers or sisters

	Frequency	%
Yes	45	77.6
No	13	22.4
Total	58	100.0

The nature of this care was varied and is indicated in Table 3.4. Practical assistance with care tasks, including dressing, feeding and toileting, and generally assisting the adult carer (e.g. fetching things) were the most cited aspects of 'care', involving nearly 41.9 per cent of activities (n = 18). Interestingly, the majority of respondents (n = 49, 81%) also felt that their non-disabled children had benefited by having a disabled brother or sister, such that sharing with caring brought positive benefits.

General 'looking after' was also frequently cited. An equally important activity was time spent entertaining and playing with the disabled sibling.

Table 3.4 Type of care

	Frequency	%
Practical assistance/care tasks	18	41.9
Looks after/baby sits	12	27.9
Plays with sibling	9	20.9
Alerts parents to things	2	4.7
Is protective	2	4.7
Total	43	100.0

Typical comments by parents included the following:

> Noticed son having seizures, getting warning from very early age. Knows what to do during an epileptic attack.

> They bath, put to bed, cook, play, supervise, toilet, prepare meals for, help clean up after, and take out.

> Helps with shopping, supervision, speaking up on behalf of their brother and looking out for him at school.

It is clearly the case that siblings help parents with the attention that was needed for the disabled child, although the extent of the caring activities varied according to the individual needs of the particular child. Helping with care was also dependent on how much responsibility the parent allowed their non-disabled child to take on:

> She helps a bit but I don't want her to have to do too much, she's not a carer.

There is no doubt that such attentions are necessary to enable the family to function. The sense of disadvantage, as used in relation to children with disabilities, is to do with being treated differently but not equally. Difference can be due to celebrity status or it can be due to a childhood perception of another child being a 'geek'. The range can be from a positive view to a negative one. The sense of disadvantage with disability is that the difference may result in being stigmatised as a group that needs special attention that goes beyond the needs of other children, such that an implicit segregation takes place. One mother summarised her view of having a disabled child thus:

I feel very lucky to have the children I have. They are all special but my boys with disabilities are extra special because of their difference and vulnerability. They make me appreciate life more – it's so easy to take things for granted if life isn't such a challenge. (Mother)

It seems apparent that living with disability brings out many desirable qualities in families, and has positive reactions from siblings and parents, but that covers over the nature of some of the limitations that families experienced. In the following case example, Ellen experiences a sense of disadvantage, mixed with a forced maturity, necessary to help her family to function.

The case of Ellen

Ellen is 14 years old. She lives with her sister Pauline (12 years old) and her father. Her mother died two years prior to interview due to ovarian cancer. Her sister Pauline has moderate learning disabilities and goes to a special school; she exhibits challenging behaviour and experiences epileptic seizures. Ellen is about to take her grade one piano exam and is very proud of her achievement. She is doing well academically but does not think she will do well enough to get to university.

At home, Pauline's bedroom is fitted with a TV camera, which is linked to the family TV in the living room and to another in the father's bedroom, so that Pauline can always be monitored when she is in her bedroom. Doors are kept locked and possessions are put 'out of reach' because Pauline may have unpredictable disruptive behaviour tantrums and/or epileptic attacks. Ellen is to have surgery to remove her ovaries because she has been assessed genetically as having a strong possibility of developing cancer in later life.

In all her activities, Ellen seems to put others before herself; she helps her father care for Pauline and assists with cooking and household chores. She has few friends because she does not have the time, and apart from schoolwork, she has found some solace in playing the piano. She appears to accept that the surgery she will undergo during her early adolescence is designed to prolong her life. Her attitudes all seem accepting of her situation and her outlook is positive – her situation fits the framework identified by Burke (2004: 53).

DISCUSSION

Ellen, it has to be said, regardless of our intent to be research objective, is a young woman whose approach to her life had some emotional impact on us both. Her maturity and understanding seem beyond her years. She seemed bright and lively despite the restrictions and isolation in her life, the latter conveying a real sense of associated disadvantage, including stigmatisation through relative neglect, social isolation and restricted future opportunity. Indeed, it seemed that given the opportunity and space, she probably could achieve the necessary grades for university entrance, but she has dismissed that possibility because she is needed at home. Ellen's disadvantage is a self-imposed restriction regarding her own future opportunities; this is a kind of self-stigmatisation reported by Paul Toh (2004) in Chapter 1. Even the opportunity to have a family of her own will not be possible due to the surgical intervention to prevent the probable occurrence of cancer. Her father works full-time and Ellen has substituted her childhood so she can be the homemaker ensuring that her sister Pauline can carry on living with the family. Pauline herself seems adjusted to her life but cannot help herself due to her behaviour and seizure activity. The family function on a day-to-day level. Ellen does not have a life of her own, her disadvantage is significant and she has accepted her situation without complaint or redress: within their confines, the family seem to be mutually supportive in meeting Pauline's needs. One can only speculate whether Ellen will react, at some point in the future, to express some form of anger at her very real restrictions; in interview, it seems that she has accepted her lot and is quietly sanguine about her future life.

The social impact of living with a disabled sibling

Many of the siblings interviewed for the study explained the restriction of activities and the associative disadvantage they had experienced including the lack of attention from parents. However, this does not provide the sense of day-to-day activities that are or are not engaged in. The simple equation is that attention is finite and that offering more in one setting deprives the opportunity in another. The following examples help to locate the family experience from the siblings' point of view, and provide examples of the social restrictions that might be encountered within a public setting.

Gloria and Emily (both aged nine) are twins. Emily was born slightly later than her sister and experienced birthing difficulties; much later she was diagnosed with autism. Emily has minor mobility difficulties and can become violent. Gloria said that outings are not easily arranged due to Emily's uncertain behaviour. Gloria explained:

> Sometimes she throws things around and she tries to hit me and my mum and scratches me and that...and she also messes things up and starts running around screaming and making a noise.

Two particular family activities that were mentioned during the study were holidays and sleepovers. These are usually normal family events but inevitably involved close supervision when a disabled child was involved. Holidays took a lot of organising, especially if special equipment was required. Sleepovers were often not practicable because friends might be disturbed by the behaviour of the disabled child:

> Because of Tom's illness [disabled child] we've not gone on family holidays. We cannot have sleepovers or watch TV in bed as the house must be quiet. Some of my friends won't visit because they don't understand. (Tom's sister)

One family that took considerable pains to arrange a holiday reported on their experience:

> We attempt a wide-range of leisure activities with our family but these are more often than not cut short due to Mark's [disabled child] inability to control his behaviour. He also has difficulty sleeping which makes us all tired as he often shouts and screams through the night. (Mother)

> I feel they have not been allowed to have a childhood. Julie's [disabled child] problems makes doing things so difficult we've been restricted as to what we can do. (Mother)

An experience that was reported by many siblings and parents was the mix of emotions induced by the people's reactions in public places. Non-disabled siblings and parents alike displayed embarrassment and anger. One parent recounted an experience with a member of the public:

> It's not just a glance...they're downright rude and will come and make comments...they'll say, 'Ooh, you're naughty aren't you?' Once I saw a woman say something to Chantelle [disabled child] and she didn't reply and she said, 'You're a naughty little girl aren't you?' And I said, 'Excuse me, she can't, she's got no language' and the woman said, 'Oh, well how was I supposed to know?' and I thought, what do they expect me to do, put a badge on her? (Parent)

For this mother, the staring by others was less frequent when her disabled child was smaller. Now that the child is older, she finds the incidents have increased, as the behaviour seems at odds with the apparent age of the child. However, the mother confesses to always assuming that people are saying negative things to her disabled child – when a woman came up to her disabled daughter and complimented her on her hair, the mother had automatically assumed the comments would be negative and managed to 'catch myself before I had a go'. In some ways this represents self-stigmatisation through association with her daughter's disability that builds on top of a sense of social disadvantage acquired from engaging in any number of similar experiences.

Non-disabled siblings experience a sense of associated disability when they were picked on in the school playground:

> Sometimes people call me a spastic and things like that but I didn't really know what it meant. I know that it means someone who's disabled. I feel upset but sometimes my friends stick up for me and say 'Did you know that my friend has a disabled sister!'

Attending the same school as a disabled brother or sister can also have an impact. One example is of a non-disabled sister having to 'step in' to support her disabled brother when non-disabled children were bullying her:

> If someone has hit Jimmy at school I'll go after them. (Pauline)

Most siblings felt that this protective role was a familial obligation and was no different from how any brother and sister would behave in school. For a minority there could sometimes be resentment:

> I always have to look out for him at school. I don't mind but if I'm with my mates then his mates come up and say if he's in a fight or something, that's a pain. (Mike)

The above typifies a sibling's sense of duty to protect his brother. This is not altogether that different to that of all siblings' sense of duty; but the sense of disadvantage when one's sibling is disabled is the one-sidedness of the exchange. Mike always has to be the defender of his disabled sibling. In the following example, a younger sister of a disabled child finds her own solutions to disability by association.

The case of Irene

Irene, now in her mid-thirties, reflected on her experience of living with an elder sister (by ten years) who has mobility difficulties. Sarah was physically disabled as a result of contracting polio as a child, at the age of seven years. The illness resulted in long spells in hospital (before Irene was born) and extensive physiotherapy was needed to help her to regain some ability in walking. Sarah had to wear callipers, attached to both legs and, now in her forties, still has difficulty with her mobility.

The issue identified by Irene, in terms of her family relationships, is the fact that for most of her early years she felt excluded within the family, because all attention centred on Sarah. Unlike John, mentioned above, Sarah was considered intellectually very bright and was doted on by her family. This had an impact on Irene in three ways:

1. Sarah needed additional attention due to her difficulties in getting out and about (thus excluding Irene)

2. Irene was considered less intellectually gifted (and was left feeling she could not achieve academically)

3. the age gap left Irene feeling she was a child in an adult family.

The consequences of these experiences made Irene feel rejected by her family; she felt her own family treated her more like an individual who had a disability herself. Irene's perceptions of her family interactions with Sarah suggested that her family almost denied Sarah's physical restrictions. Irene said she had to deal with feelings of rejection in her own family, in thinking she must, in some way, be disabled herself, a situation she sought to resolve. Her solution was to avoid engaging with her own family, because she said 'they were a hopeless case'. Instead, she turned to another family in seeking the support and help she felt had been denied at home. Once again this fits the image of disadvantage as a form of neglect, of stigmatisation by social elements in the home, or, in another sense, acquiring a 'spoiled identity' (Goffman, 1963).

DISCUSSION

Irene's case illustrates that she felt disadvantaged in her relationship with her disabled sister and identified with disability herself, as thought she too carried part of her sister's disability. In terms of the adjustment (Burke, 2004: 33) it would appear that her reaction was one of anger, resulting in her rejection of her birth family in substituting another. For Irene this worked very well and she explained that, although she has always kept in touch with her birth family, she went on her own way and achieved degree-level qualifications on par with her disabled sister and always felt and was treated as second best. Her sister's needs still appear to come first in family relationships and, through time, have become set and unmovable. It seems that whatever the response might be to disability, adjustments are partial and individuals accept their place in family relationships. Disability by association become part of that make-up, as this and the earlier research by Burke (2004) will testify.

Conclusion on associative conditions in siblings

It was hypothesised that the nature of disability by association may change over time and therefore was not 'fixed' by one typical response as appeared to be indicated in the earlier research (Burke, 2004; Burke and Cigno, 1996). The results from this research appear to support the view that 'disability by association' does exist as a socially constructed experience.

However, it seems that living with disability does appear to 'fix' a type of response on the part of siblings: siblings learn how to deal with the conditions and experiences that link with living with a brother or sister who has a disability, as a way of coming to terms with the world.

It is the case that disability becomes part of the family's strength, its identity, and that promotes a defence against other social institutions or engagements, which seems to be a consequence of such experiences. The reactions to 'disability by association' seem entrenched, and continuing encounters with stigmatising elements do appear to reinforce a defensive position. However, although this may seem a 'typical' reaction we note that parents (over 80%) felt that their non-disabled children benefited from having a disabled brother or sister, this benefit being in terms of reaching an understanding and maturity beyond their chronological years. The need for social work to engage with siblings is apparent, although it appears to be a societal condition that constructs disability beyond impairment. This needs greater understanding if the barriers that exclude disabled people and those associated with them are to be dismantled.

References

Bridge, G. (1999) *Parents as Care Managers*. Aldershot: Ashgate.

Burke, P. (2004) *Brothers and Sisters of Disabled Children*. London: Jessica Kingsley Publishers.

Burke, P. (2005) 'Listening to young people with special needs: The influence of group activities.' *Journal of Intellectual Disabilities 9*, 4, 359–76.

Burke, P. and Cigno, K. (1996) *Support for Families: Helping Children with Learning Disabilities*. Aldershot: Ashgate.

Burke, P. and Cigno, K. (2000) *Learning Disabilities in Children*. Oxford: Blackwell Science.

Burke, P. and Montgomery, S. (2001) 'Brothers and sisters: supporting the siblings of children with disabilities.' *Practice 13*, 1, 27–36.

Burke, P. and Montgomery, S. (2003) *Finding a Voice*. Birmingham: Ventura Press.

Darlington, Y. and Scott, S. (2002) *Qualitative Research in Practice: Stories from the Field*. Buckingham: Open University Press.

Goffman, E. (1963) *Stigma, Notes on the Management of Spoilt Identity*. London: Penguin.

Greene, S. and Hill, M. (2005) 'Conceptual, Methodological and Ethical Issues in Researching Children's Experience.' In S. Greene and D. Hogan (eds) *Researching Children's Experience: Methods and Approaches*. London: Sage.

Grinyer, A. (2002) 'The anonymity of research participants: assumptions, ethics and practicalities.' *Social Research Update 36*, 1–4.

Hopson, B. (1981) 'Transitions, Understanding and Managing Personal Change.' In M. Herbert (ed.) *Psychology for Social Workers*. London: Macmillan.

Joseph Rowntree Foundation (1999) Findings of Report N79. Available at www.jrf.org.uk/knowledge (accessed 2006).

Kübler Ross, E. (1969) *On Death and Dying*. London: Tavistock.

Malin, N.A. and Wilmot, S. (2000) 'An ethical advisory group in a learning disability service: what they talk about.' *Journal of Learning Disabilities 4*, 3, 217–26.

Ramcharan, P. and Cutcliffe, J. (2001) 'Judging the ethics of qualitative research.' *Health and Social Care in the Community 9*, 6, 358–66.

Toh, P. (2004) *Personal Experiences, HIV and Self-Stigma, Summary of Stigma Aids eForum discussion*. HDN, www.hdnet.org (accessed March 2006).

Chapter 4

A Drug User in the Family: Between Need, Dependency and Desire

Philip Guy

This chapter is about drug use, the family and social exclusion. Problematic drug use is one of the most troubling issues in contemporary social life. Those who take drugs are often socially excluded through the legal process. This notion becomes less opaque when the words are rearranged. Drug users are excluded from society. This occurs in a number of ways but most obviously when, despite having extensive welfare needs, users are sent to prison for drug possession. No other client group represented in this book suffers this fate. In a society dominated by mass communication it seems, for example, that no film-maker, script writer, novelist or journalist seeks to portray drug users outside of a wholly negative stereotype. Readers might like to consider whether they think this fate is justified when they have read this chapter.

Those who care for drug users often find themselves stigmatised through association, excluded at a social level through the loss of intimacy with wider family and friends and excluded institutionally through not receiving the support they need. In order to explore these issues research findings about the causal relationship between childhood experiences and problematic drug use will be outlined, together with some findings on how the optimum outcomes from treatment can be obtained. There are two sides to this issue. Research says clearly that families, and the poor quality parenting they sometimes provide, are part of the problem. Conversely, the support that families can give their drug-using children can improve significantly the outcomes of professional help. Families therefore sit in a precarious position within this issue. They often suffer the true impact of drug use and attract a stigma, yet they have the resources that can make all the difference to the user.

In this chapter the impact that drug use has on family life will also be considered. The role that families can play in supporting their drug-using members will be outlined and the stigma of being a drug user's parent and how this stigma might be overcome will be discussed. Children are always a focus of concern for social workers; here, however, it is not the intention to repeat work that has focused on the impact of parental drug use on family life and the welfare of children.

A drug-using culture: An excluding society

The social change that underpins this issue is a simple but often overlooked one. Over the past four decades drug-trying in the UK has risen by an amount few would have predicted (Guy and Harrison, 2003). The social work profession has barely kept pace with the massive cultural change in attitudes towards drugs. Drug use is, if not statistically normal, acceptable and practised by a large subsection of society (6, Jup and Laskey, 1997; Parker, Aldridge and Egginton, 2001; Parker, Aldridge and Measham, 1998; Wibberley and Price, 2000). Drug users can now be found amongst most client groups (Guy and Harrison, 2003).

Estimates derived from the British Crime Survey suggest that there are four million regular users of illicit drugs in the UK (Condon and Smith, 2003). If we take a cautious view and suggest that each drug user will negatively affect two other people through their drug use there may be over eight million people in the UK for whom family drug use is an issue. The main policy response, sometimes called 'a war on drugs', and the rhetoric that surrounds it cast the drug users as removed by their habit from society, family and friends (Guy, 2005). This discourse serves the needs of prohibition and enforcement rather than a welfare agenda partly because it says nothing about why people use drugs in the first place. Buchanan (2004), however, suggests that an underlying if not causal relationship exists between social exclusion and drug use:

> A disproportionate number of problem drug users have been disadvantaged and socially excluded prior to taking drugs. For many the all-consuming drug-centred lifestyle is the only adult existence they have known and should be seen as an inappropriate solution, rather than the problem itself. (Buchanan, 2004: 396)

There is a sad irony to Buchanan's conclusion. Usually, it is said that drug use makes things worse for the user because of the drug's chemical properties. However, it is clear that once adopted as a lifestyle, drug use increases the user's social exclusion for social and political reasons.

As Mach (2002) points out, one of the historical strands of social exclusion as a concept originated in the social policies of Nazi Germany. Contemporary commentators use the term 'social exclusion' as if the process is unintentional, unfortunate and often the result of the way in which wealth is distributed in society. In Nazi Germany, however, the intention was to deliberately exclude all of the people whose lives revolve around the kind of issues that this book is about. They, along with drug users, were systematically separated, sterilised, forced into slavery and murdered. The rationale for this was the view that the people that social workers work with are a contagion that should be separated from society, for society's good. Mach demonstrates how, in order to exclude drug users, the Nazi state adopted a practice of vilification through language, negative associations and graphic images that separated drug users out from the rest of society:

> These claims were congruent with a definition of drug use, not as a lifestyle, but rather as the symptom of an 'addicted personality', which in turn, indicated 'genetic inferiority.' Drug users were labelled 'asocial,' escaping their 'national obligations' and 'sinning against the common interest...' (Mach, 2002: 381)

No one would claim that in contemporary UK society vulnerable people suffer a fate as serious as this. As Mach says:

> The objective and agendas of political ideology based on and fostering social exclusion is hardly imaginable anymore... It is clear that the limits of legitimate social expression are not nearly as narrow as they once were. Actual exclusions have become relatively rare and are difficult to explain and legitimize when they occur... (Mach, 2002: 378)

However, attitudes towards drug users have not moved on as much as might be expected and drug users are socially excluded as a matter of policy. Moreover, social exclusion cannot be neatly limited to drug users as if it were a fitted carpet the extent of which could be controlled; rather it extends to the families and carers of drug users as well.

Despite the current situation the UK has a long history of viewing drug use as a welfare issue. During the 1930s and 1940s when the Nazis were persecuting drug users, the UK was offering humane treatment and rehabilitation. The turning point came in the late 1960s and was given legitimacy under The Misuse of Drugs Act (HMSO 1971) (Maclean, 1985). Since this time welfare has been subsumed under the political rhetoric of a 'war on drugs'. The drug policies of New Labour are no different in this respect. They follow a trend set out three decades ago and are increasingly punitive and coercive in both tone and intention (Buchanan, 2004; Buchanan and Young, 2000).

However, despite the rhetoric, public image and the intention of policy, drug use is not necessarily an isolated or isolating activity. It is usually carried out in groups or in the company of others (Parker *et al.*, 1998; Power and Jones, 1995). Moreover, drug users are usually to be found living in family situations (Forsyth and Barnard, 2003). In other words, like other excluded groups drug users tend to stick together. Csiernik (2002) suggests that by the time a drug user seeks treatment the impact of their drug use will be felt by all of the family members. Moreover, whilst dying alone and in considerable squalor is a popular stereotype of a drug user's death, the family home is the most usual site for such tragic events, and family and friends are likely to witness them (ACMD, 2000).

While the maximum sentence of seven years for the possession of a class (A) drug tells society that drug users are criminals who should be excluded from society, families take on the role of caring and actually live with, and love, those society has labelled deviant. The gap between the rhetoric and the reality is an obvious one. As carers they are excluded from receiving recognition of their own needs and an understanding of their contribution to the care of drug users. Whatever is said on this topic, family carers still carry much of the real impact that drug use can have.

Coping with someone else's drug use

It is possible to have a son or daughter with a large drug habit living in the family home and for parents and siblings to be completely unaware of this activity. In view of what follows this might be considered a comfortable situation. However, when things go wrong finding out can be a profoundly disturbing process (Guy, 2004). Research consistently suggests that the impact that a family member's drug use has on the other family members is a negative one. As the Scottish Executive Effective Interventions Unit recently pointed out, whether the user regards their drug use as a problem or not, amongst other family members drug use can generate a considerable amount of anxiety and family discord:

> It was clear from across the studies that the experience of living with drug use in the family produces a great deal of stress leading to a range of physical and psychological health problems. The literature review identified research on short-term effects which include anxiety, guilt, loneliness, worry, fear and confusion. Longer-term effects include significant physical ailments such as shingles, ulcers, raised blood pressure and psychological problems such as depression, panic attacks and anxiety disorders. (EIU, undated: 10)

Faced with this stress it is worthwhile remembering that those who care for drug users, unlike the professionals involved, did not volunteer for the role. Indeed, it is apparent that many do not take on the role and that this is detrimental to the drug users' well-being. For example, in a sample of homeless people with substance problems in London, Fountain *et al.* (2003) found that amongst those who believed that their substance use was the cause of their homelessness, 58 per cent also highlighted problems with parents. If these problems had been resolved and the drug user had been able to stay in the family home, the outcome from any treatment intervention would be likely to have been far better (Guy and Harrison, 2003; McCarthy and Galvani, 2004). In the absence of an inclusive approach to these issues, and the opportunity to access honest information, help in clarifying the carer's role and support in providing a clear and consistent approach to their drug-using family members, a valuable resource has been lost. For many others, caring is a duty carried out for love in the certain knowledge that no one else will do it.

Stewart (1987) makes an important point about the stage of life that parents might feel they should be enjoying and the unwanted challenges that drug use can bring. Stewart starts by pointing out that the parental role with small children is the usual and expected one. The needs of young children and a parent's role in raising them are understood by all but the most inadequate parents. However, as Stewart points out, this role is less clear when children grow up. Moreover, caring for drug-using children who are adults is a new and unexpected parenting task that comes at a time when it is less welcome:

> Just when the job of bringing them up seemed to be over, when the worry and struggle seemed likely to end, the situation becomes worse than it ever was. Parents must get ready to cope with conflict, aggression, instability, upheaval, disappointment and real fears for the safety and welfare of their son or daughter. (Stewart, 1987: 139–40)

Perry 6 and his colleagues also suggest that young problem users, for their part, also experience family life negatively. They report a less trusting relationship between parent and offspring with drug use often being the focus of this distrust (6 *et al.*, 1997: 17). Velleman *et al.*'s (1993) research goes some way to explaining this distrust. They suggest that the presence of a drug user in a family presents parents and siblings with a dilemma in which there is no obvious or agreed way of dealing with the situation.

Families in this situation are working whilst excluded from support. They are also caring without an instruction book, unaware of the nature of drug use or how to respond. The wider family and friends may be in the same situation, having no experience in such matters themselves. Moreover, given the stigma attached to drug use, carers may feel unable to approach them. Help from a specialist agency may be available in some areas and it has been shown that working with families can significantly reduce the stress of caring for a drug user (Butler and Bauld, 2005; Copello and Orford, 2002; EIU, undated). However, research conducted by Evans, Mallick and Stein (1998) suggests that 76.5 per cent of parents are not aware of the services in their area that can offer help.

The approach taken by families, Velleman *et al.* (1993) suggests, often swings inconsistently between soft, conciliatory attempts to understand and help and a firm, hard-line stand against the drug use. On the other side of the relationship drug users also experience the negative impact that such inconsistency and uncertainty can bring (Quigley, 2002). McCambridge and Strang (2004) found that 40 per cent of the drug users they surveyed reported interactive difficulties with others, most often parents. The younger the respondent the more likely they were to report such issues.

As the parents' values about drug use are openly challenged and they find themselves with family duties connected to drug use like, for example, visiting a son in prison, they often feel a deep sense of their own failure (Butler and Bauld, 2005; Guy, 2004). Lockley (1996) describes families in which the relationship between parents becomes strained as they attempt to cope with the offspring's drug use. The drug-using family member often starts to dominate family life. Lockley suggests that they become the only family member acting in what they believe to be their own self-interest. In this situation, Lockley argues, the rest of the family fall in line, afraid to upset whatever delicate equilibrium exists, subjugating their needs and desires to those of the user.

The Scottish Executive Effective Interventions Unit suggested that some parents, feeling that it was the only way of keeping their children safe, resorted to buying illicit drugs for them themselves. This, however, often combined with the problems that were experienced in trying to care and remain an effective employee, compounded the family's financial problems:

> financial difficulties were increased because family members had given up working. They felt unable to cope with the demands of work and the stress resulting from drug use in the family. Over half of the respondents to the conference survey had experienced difficulties at work because of the impact of drug use on the family. (EIU undated: 11)

Purchasing drugs for someone else, no matter how well intended, is an offence under The Misuse of Drugs Act (1971) that can lead to up to 21 years in prison if the drug is in class (A), for example heroin or cocaine. What lies behind the desperation that leads to law breaking, risk of prosecution and a deep conflict with personal values is the fear of the very worst outcome, the death of a loved one.

Nevertheless, despite the large numbers of people who use illicit drugs, comparatively few people will experience bereavement through this cause. In a population of 300,000 people the Audit Commission (2004: 5) suggest that ten deaths per year will be drug related. However, in a research project to try and understand the experience of bereavement through drug use (Guy, 2004), it was found that death was a constant worry for those looking after drug users. Death forms the main message of anti-drug campaigns. So it is not surprising that the risk of death overshadowed family life far more than the actual likelihood of it occurring would seem to warrant. It was this fear that lay behind many arguments between parents and between parents and their child. It was also this fear that lay behind many family breakdowns and the loss of a secure source of support.

When loved ones died those deaths often occurred during periods of comparative optimism when parents thought their arguments had been heard and their son or daughter had stopped or moderated their drug use. Expecting the worst and then experiencing it at a time when the issues seemed almost resolved seems for many to be a double blow. Death brought no respite from feelings of inadequacy and, as in life, the emotional turmoil that came with death was denied legitimacy by wider society (Guy, 2004). The grief that parents felt was particularly long lasting and parents were often unable to make sense of their loss years later. The feeling that grief for someone who has been labelled deviant by society is not legitimate grief exacerbated the feelings of loss and failure. Thus stigma by association and social exclusion by association continued beyond life.

The stigma of being seen as a poor parent
Given the difficulties, arguments and discord that seem to accompany a drug user in the family it would not be surprising if parents who persist with the task of caring, often without any of the positive rewards normally attached to the role, start to feel unworthy and inadequate. They may also feel that a drug user in the family is, in itself, a sign of their inadequacy, and that others will believe this too:

> the difficulties associated with drug use in the family frequently had an impact on the social lives of family members. For some in the qualitative study, the stigma that can be associated with drug use and their own embarrassment about the situation had led to increased isolation from extended family and friends. For others, it was the practical demands of

> dealing with all the problems associated with drug use that had prevented
> them maintaining social contacts. (EIU, undated: 12)

Many people in this situation feel alienated from wider family and friends. They often report that they feel others are talking about them (EIU, undated; Guy, 2004).The usual way of viewing this kind of stigma by association is provided by Goffman (1963). Predominantly, Goffman's ideas on stigma are interpreted in a way that suggests that those who take on stigma by association do so by default, as if the status is undeserved. However, the parents of drug users do not necessarily occupy such clear-cut ground and may become stigmatised far more easily. Drug use has such strong family associations for many that this may provide further reasons why the parents of drug users may feel uncomfortable or even guilty about their offspring's drug use and their role in it, not least because much research has been focused on the role of parents in the antecedence of that drug use.

Research into the antecedence of drug use suggests that in societies where drugs are easily available, the structure of the family and the quality of relationships may be an important issue (McArdle *et al.*, 2002; Quensel *et al.*, 2002). For males, McArdle *et al.* suggest that living with both parents and having a good relationship with the mother may be protective factors. The United Nations (2000: 119) argue that there is a skills deficit in families where children take drugs. They suggest that there is a need to improve parenting as a preventative measure. This implication places the cause of drug use firmly on the actions or inactions of parents.

When research focuses on the actions of parents a reason for their stigmatisation beyond the stigma attached to drug use itself becomes apparent. Downs and Harrison (1998), Velleman and Orford (1998) and Quigley (2002) highlight the prevalence of problematic parental drinking in the background of young drug users. Quigley (2002) moves these findings on into familiar social work issues. He describes the complex family background of a sample of drug users in treatment where periods of foster care or institutional living were not uncommon, and nor were parental substance problems and inconsistent and poor parenting:

> The most common stereotypes reported were the binge-drinking father,
> perhaps regularly engaged in domestic violence, and the mother who was
> dependent on prescription sedatives. Sexual assault within the extended
> family was reported by a significant minority. (Quigley, 2002: 224)

Being a treatment sample it could be argued that Quigley's findings may have come from the extreme end of a continuum. However, samples taken from the general population tend to confirm the negative role that parents play in the development of a drug-using career. Perez, for example, is not saying that parents perpetrated the negative experiences that were found amongst her sample of young people; nevertheless the implication is there:

> overall, physical abuse, sexual victimization, and the co-occurrence of both types of abuse were significantly related to higher levels of illicit drug use. The odds of reporting higher levels of past month marijuana use for physically abused youth were 56% greater than the odds for non-physically abused youth, other things being equal... (Perez, 2000: 650)

Research like this may produce a dilemma for the practitioner because it highlights, either through unintended deficits or wilful abuse, the role of poor parenting in the development of a drug problem. Yet, at the same time, other research also highlights the value of parents in supporting drug users towards healthier lifestyles. The research does not suggest that those who have provided poor parenting are the same parents who work tirelessly in support of their drug-using children; indeed, this seems unlikely. The research does not make such fine distinctions between good parents and bad parents. Moreover, the social mechanisms that assign stigmatisation and underpin the experience of it also do not differentiate between the good and the bad. For parents, being seen as part of the problem and yet also being given an unexpected and unwanted part in the solution is personally debilitating.

Discussion
One of the underlying factors behind this book is that a reappraisal of the social situation many clients occupy has taken place. As a result of this social workers have become far more aware of the role of carers. Those who care in a wide variety of situations have gradually received recognition from the profession and have had their needs placed firmly on the social work agenda, for example young carers (Frank, 2002) and those who work and also care for older adults (Philips, Bernard and Chittenden, 2002). Research has recognised the vital nature of the family, outlining the role of the carer and the contribution that they make to the care of the vulnerable, as well as their need for support in this task.

The Carers (Recognition and Services) Act (HMSO, 1995) formally recognised those who provide care to relatives and friends. A carer can request an assessment of their own needs if, under community care legislation, the person for whom they care is eligible for assessment. When making decisions about the services local authorities have to consider the result of the carer's assessment. Nevertheless, despite these clear advances those who have drug users in their families have not generally been part of this movement (Butler and Bauld, 2005; EIU, undated). Carers of drug users can feel isolated and socially excluded and for those whose role remains unrecognised this is all the more so. They remain largely excluded at an institutional level from the help and support that others may receive, as the Scottish Executive Effective Interventions point out:

> Family members involved in caring for drug users or their dependents often report that they do not see themselves as 'carers' and as a result perceive that they have few rights. This appears to be reinforced by an analysis of publicity and information on carers' organisations. (EIU, undated: 19)

That families feel this way and regard themselves as just coping rather than caring may be a reflection of the stress they are under or a view about their own competence. Policy-makers and practitioners may share some of these views. Given the research evidence it is not surprising that suspicion sometimes surrounds the parenting abilities of those whose children use drugs. It also seems that a conception of the drug user as vulnerable, and an understanding that there may be those who care for them, is an anathema in the war against drugs and the demonisation of drug users. This is most unfortunate given the body of work that concludes that the outcomes of professional interventions depend closely on the level of support that a drug user receives from family and close friends (ACMD, 1999; Andersen and Berg, 2001; Butler and Bauld, 2005; Copello and Orford, 2002; Dobkin et al., 2001; McCarthy and Galvani, 2004).

Copello and Orford summarise the limited acceptance of the needs of families and their role as carers within the field:

> Evidence is therefore growing to support the view that families and social networks can be influential, yet a paradox is evident when we look at addiction services. Despite the accumulating evidence for the important role of families, on the whole service delivery remains focused on the individual drinker or drug user, with families and other members of the users social network playing a very peripheral role if any. (Copello and Orford, 2002: 1361)

Part of the anxiety that families feel when faced with drug use stems from being left alone to care and work things out for themselves. A lack of knowledge about drugs and drug use also compounds this anxiety (Butler and Bauld, 2005). This is a form of social exclusion in itself. This lack of knowledge is fuelled by a well-meaning, but negative, portrayal of drug use and drug users. It is through these portrayals and the stark images they use that the stigma attached to drug users and those who care for them draws much of its power (Guy, 2005). By showing young people what can happen when drugs are taken it is often believed that they will be dissuaded from taking the practice up and those already using will stop. Although it is not an idea derived from research, the shock message has a long lineage in anti-drug campaigns. The shock message requires graphic imagery to represent a worse case scenario. In this sense the lineage of many of the methods used in contemporary anti-drug campaigns can be traced back to the propaganda that justified social exclusion in Nazi Germany (Burleigh, 1994; Mach, 2002).

The tag line, 'Heroin screws you up', under a squalid image of an emaciated user provided the shock message in the 1980s (Davenport-Hines, 2001). There have been many such incidents since with newspapers in particular vying for the most sensational headline and graphic imagery (Guy, 2004). A more recent campaign by the Metropolitan Police (Cowan, 2004; Roberts, 2004) took the form of a series of photographs of women claiming to show the cumulative impact of drug use. This is how Cowan describes the campaign:

> Haunting Police mug shots of three American addicts show their decline over a few years, from healthy women to skeletal figures with wizened faces and sunken eyes. The pictures were taken when the women were arrested for drug related crimes and have been provided by US police departments. (Cowan, 2004: 6)

So marginalised and socially excluded are the families of drug users that few people stop to consider how they might receive this kind of message. The point is a significant one. It is often the fear that parents have rather than what actually happens that can dominate family relationships (Shewan and Dalgarno, 2005). What is missing is an understanding that shock campaigns may also shock and unnecessarily alarm carers. If this is what happens to drug users then the future for any son or daughter seems inevitable. The pictures give the misleading impression that drug use is inexorably connected to crime and physical decline. Parents will not be aware that most drug users are otherwise law-abiding citizens (Parker et al., 1998; 6 et al., 1997), or that many will lead relatively normal lives (Shewan and Dalgarno, 2005). Parents will also not be aware that the photographs were taken in a country that has a death rate from illicit drug overdose that is three times higher than in Europe (United Nations, 2000: 99).

One thing that will occur from such messages is that drug users are seen as rejecting us, and our norms and values, and so it becomes easier for us to reject them (Guy, 2005). Thus, stigma and social exclusion go hand in hand, and other biographical possibilities about drug users do not get raised in popular discourse. Whatever the intended outcome the possibility that drug users would like to be like us, or how they imagine we are, will be denied. The insight that drug use might help the user hide from the thoughts and feelings that prevent normality will be apparent to only a few.

The thoughts and feelings of families are also unlikely to have been uppermost in the campaign designer's mind. To see these images when one is anxious about a loved one cannot be pleasant. It may be that the social exclusion of drug users requires stark, uncompromising images that have been chosen to emphasise deviance and shock. It seems highly unlikely that a portrayal like this one of any other client group would be regarded as acceptable.

Something of the sea change that will necessarily occur if the role and needs of families are placed firmly on the social work agenda will be appreciated if consideration is given to the ways in which social work practice with substance-using parents has changed, as it has become a more common casework concern.

Over the last decade child protection practice has moved from one that usually did no more that separate child from parents (Taylor, 1993). It is now recognised that family breakdown has problems of its own. This has caused a reappraisal of the notion that drug-using parents are necessarily bad parents who should be excluded from the role. Now the first consideration is how the family might be supported in staying together in a way that will enable the parents to improve their performance (Adams, 1999). There is every reason to believe that when the situation is reversed and it is the children who are using drugs the same approach would be beneficial. Strategies that would help families stay together have a potential of immense welfare value. If all fails and families break up, strategies that help to keep families in touch could be underpinned by strategies to bring families back together, particularly when young people most need family support and help.

To be of help to their drug-using members the families of drug users need to overcome the social stigma that is attached to drug use and being the parent of a drug user. To achieve this they will then need a consistent strategy that is underpinned by social work support. For their part, social workers will have to acknowledge the value of family support as the vital underpinning to interventions and where the family links are broken seek to re-establish them.

The difficulties that a family face, and that social work may have to assist with, might seem surprising given the positive contribution that families can make to the welfare of drug-using family members. Working with families has been shown to have positive outcomes for alcohol users even when they do not acknowledge a problem and are not prepared to come forward for help themselves (Miller *et al.*, 1999). For those in touch with treatment services social support is associated with an elevated likelihood that the drug user will be retained in treatment longer. This is known to be a factor in good outcomes as Dobkin *et al.* (2001) point out:

> The benefits of treatment adherence may include gaining mastery over the urge to use, learning how to negotiate risky situations and developing a repertoire of coping strategies to deal with the difficulties encountered during the early stages of recovery. (Dobkin *et al.*, 2001: 355)

Widely used theoretical models in social work practice like the Transtheoretical Model of Change (Prochasca and DiClemente 1986), tend to view the individual and the decisions they make in splendid isolation from family and friends. In order to bridge the gap between current practice and research on good outcomes new ways of thinking and working will have to be found. More recent and arguably more useful models, like McCarthy's SCARS (McCarthy and Galvani, 2004), suggest that for the optimum outcome from a treatment intervention aimed at assisting drug users in change a further five elements must be in place:

> Underpinning the SCARS model is the evidence base that suggests that successful substance treatment outcomes are optimised when other key aspects (typically referred to as 'protective factors' or 'resilience factors') of the individual's well-being and environment are secure. (McCarthy and Galvani, 2004: 89)

The key elements in addition to addictions treatment identified by McCarthy and Galvani are accommodation, employment, physical health, psychological health and significant relationships. All of these elements are associated with family life. The absence of all of these elements is a feature of social exclusion. This should place social work with drug users firmly within a family orientation and recognise the vital role that families play as carers.

Conclusion

Problem drug use is one of the most pressing social problems of our times. Despite all the emphasis in criminal law and anti-drug campaigns, arguably it is the families of drug users who suffer the most. Drug use puts considerable strain on families; they are its forgotten victims. Part of this strain is derived from the wedge that the demonisation of drug use drives between family members. Families carry the cost of drug use in a situation where advice and support are difficult to come by.

Many drug problems have their origins in poor parenting. Yet at the same time the family is a vital component of the support that drug users need for a successful outcome. This paradox needs to be understood if professional views and service provision are to be reshaped.

Society has rejected drug use and drug users and while this is the case those who care for them will always be at risk from social exclusion and stigma. Social work has been slow in responding to this form of social exclusion yet it can do much to challenge the longstanding perception that drives policy and practice.

Drug use is strongly associated with social exclusion and a range of individual and social problems. However, there is an element of this exclusion that is not the result of happenchance or some complex, hidden social mechanism. One of the strands that make up the origins of social exclusion as a concept is related directly to the social policies of Nazi Germany. This was one of the darkest periods of human history. Knowledge of this point should be enough to alert us to the dangers of policies that set out deliberately to exclude those in need from the rest of society.

The deliberate creation of social exclusion and its extension by association to families is part of the problem. Such policies are not beyond question and not beyond change. This chapter has provided some good reasons why policy should be focused on inclusion rather than exclusion. If the current policies were successful we would not be where we are today.

References

ACMD (1999) Advisory Counsel on the Misuse of Drugs. *Drug Use and the Environment.* London: HMSO.

ACMD (2000) Advisory Counsel on the Misuse of Drugs. *Reducing Drug Related Deaths.* London: HMSO.

Adams, P. (1999) 'Towards a family support approach with drug using parents: the importance of social worker attitudes and knowledge.' *Child Abuse Review 8,* 15–28.

Andersen, S. and Berg, J. (2001) 'The use of a sense of coherence test to predict drop-out and mortality after residential treatment of substance abuse.' *Addiction Research and Theory 9,* 3, 239–51.

Audit Commission (2004) *Drug Misuse 2004 Reducing the Local Impact.* London: Audit Commission.

Buchanan, J. (2004) 'Missing links? Problem drug use and social exclusion.' *Probation Journal, the Journal of Community and Criminal Justice 51,* 4, 387–97.

Buchanan, J. and Young, L. (2000) 'The war on drugs: a war on drug users?' *Drugs: Education, Prevention and Policy 7,* 4, 409–22.

Burleigh, M. (1994) *Death and Deliverance 'Euthanasia' in Germany 1900–1945.* Cambridge: Cambridge University Press.

Butler, R. and Bauld, L. (2005) 'The parents' experience: coping with drug use in the family.' *Drugs: Education, Prevention and Policy 12,* 1, 35–46.

Condon, J. and Smith, N. (2003) *Prevalence of Drug Use: Key Findings from the 2002/2003 British Crime Survey. Home Office Findings 229.* London: HMSO.

Copello, A. and Orford, J. (2002) 'Addiction and the family: is it time for services to take notice of the evidence?' *Addictions 97*, 1361–3.

Cowan, R. (2004) Police Photo Campaign Shows Ravages of Addiction. Shock Tactics Aimed At Encouraging Informants. *Guardian*, 2 November.

Csiernik, R. (2002) 'Counselling for the family: the neglected aspect of addiction treatment in Canada.' *Journal of Social Work in the Addictions 2*, 1, 79–92.

Davenport-Hines, R. (2001) *The Pursuit of Oblivion: A Global History of Narcotics 1500–2000*. London: Weidenfeld & Nicolson.

Dobkin, P., De Civita, M., Paraherakis, A. and Gill, K. (2001) 'The role of functional support in treatment outcomes among adult substance abusers.' *Addictions 97*, 347–56.

Downs, W.R. and Harrison, L. (1998) 'Childhood maltreatment and the risk of substance problems in later life.' *Health and Social Care in the Community 6*, 1, 35–46.

EIU (undated) *Supporting Families and Carers of Drug Users: A Review*. Edinburgh: The Scottish Executive Effective Interventions Unit.

Evans, R., Mallick, J. and Stein, G. (1998) 'The Role of Parents in Drug Education.' In L. O'Connor, D. O'Connor and R. Best (eds) *Drugs: Partnerships for Policy, Prevention and Education*. London: Cassell.

Forsyth, A. and Barnard, M. (2003) 'Young people's awareness of illicit drug use in the family.' *Addiction Research and Theory 11*, 6, 459–72.

Fountain, J., Howes, S., Marsden, J., Taylor, C. and Strang, J. (2003) 'Drug and alcohol use and the link with homelessness: results from a survey of homeless people in London.' *Addiction Research and Theory 11*, 4, 245–56.

Frank, J. (2002) *Making it Work: Good Practice with Young Carers and their Families*. London: The Children's Society and The Princess Royal Trust for Carers.

Goffman, E. (1963) *Stigma: Notes on a Spoiled Identity*. London: Penguin.

Guy, P. (2004) 'Bereavement through drug use: messages from research.' *Practice 16*, 1, 43–54.

Guy, P. (2005) 'Dope Fiends: The Myth and Menace of Drug Users in Film.' In M. King and K. Watson (eds) *Representing Health. Discourses of Health and Illness in the Media*. Basingstoke: Palgrave Macmillan.

Guy, P. and Harrison, L. (2003) 'Evidence Based Work with People who have Substance Problems.' In J. Horwath and S.M. Shardlow (eds) *Making Links Across Specialisms: Understanding Modern Social Work Practice*. Lyme Regis: Russell House.

HMSO (1971) The Misuse of Drugs Act. London: HMSO.

HMSO (1995) The Carers (Recognition and Services) Act. London: HMSO. Available at: www.hmso.gov.uk/acts/acts1995/Ukpga_19950012_en_1.htm (accessed June 2005).

Lockley, P. (1996) *Working with Drug Family Support Groups*. London: Free Association Books.

Mach, H. (2002) 'Exclusion and extinction. The fight against narcotics in the third reich.' *Journal of Drug Issues 31*, 2, 379–94.

Maclean, E. (1985) 'Official Responses to Drugs and Drug Dependence.' In J. Lishman (ed.) *Approaches to Addiction: Research Highlight in Social Work, 10*. London: Kogan Page.

McArdle, P., Wiegersma, A., Gilvarry, A., Kolte, B., McCarthy, S., Fitzgerald, M., Brinkley, A., Blom, M., Stoeckel, I., Pierolini, A., Michels, I., Johnson, R. and Quensel, S. (2002) 'European adolescent substance use: the roles of family structure, function and gender.' *Addiction 97*, 329–36.

McCambridge, J. and Strang, J. (2004) 'Drug problem – what problems? Concurrent predictors of selected types of drug problems in a London community sample of young people who use drugs.' *Addiction Research and Theory 12*, 1, 55–66.

McCarthy, T. and Galvani, S, (2004) 'SCARS: A new approach for working with substance users.' *Practice 16*, 2, 85–97.

Miller, W.R., Meyers, R.J. and Tonigen, J.S. (1999) 'Engaging the unmotivated in treatment for alcohol problems.' *Journal of Consulting Psychology 67*, 4, 688–97.

Parker, H., Aldridge, J. and Egginton, R. (2001) *UK Drugs Unlimited: New Research and Policy Lessons on Illicit Drug Use.* Basingstoke: Palgrave Macmillan.

Parker, H., Aldridge, J. and Measham, F. (1998) *Illegal Leisure: The Normalisation of Adolescent Recreational Drug Use.* London: Routledge.

Perez, D. (2000) 'The relationship between physical abuse, sexual victimization, and adolescent illicit drug use.' *Journal of Drug Issues 30,* 3, 641–62.

Philips, J., Bernard, M. and Chittenden, M. (2002) *Juggling Work and Care: The Experiences of Working Carers of Older Adults.* Bristol: The Policy Press.

Power, R. and Jones, S. (1995) *Coping with Illicit Drug Use.* London: Tufnell Press.

Prochaska, J. and DiClemente, C. (1986) 'Toward a Comprehensive Model of Change.' In W.R. Miller and H. Heather (eds) *Treating Addictive Behaviours.* New York: Plenum Press.

Quensel, S., McArdla, P., Brinkley, A., Wiegersma, A. with Blom, M., Fitzgerald, M., Johnson, R., Kolte, B., Michels, I., Pierollini, A., Pos, R. and Stoeckel, I. (2002) 'Broken home or drug using peers: "significant relations"?' *Journal of Drug Issues 32,* 2, 467–90.

Quigley, P. (2002) 'Family and community burdens of addiction: case-mix analysis at a new community-based methadone treatment.' *Drugs: Education, Prevention and Policy 9,* 3, 221–31.

Roberts, Y. (2004) Face Value. *Guardian,* 4 November.

Shewan, D. and Dalgarno, P. (2005) 'Low levels of negative health and social outcomes among non-treatment heroin users in Glasgow (Scotland): evidence for controlled heroin use?' *British Journal of Health Psychology 10,* 1–17.

6, P., Jup, B. and Laskey, K. (1997) *The Substance of Youth: The Role of Drugs in Young People's Lives Today.* York: Joseph Rowntree Foundation.

Stewart, T. (1987) *The Heroin Users.* London: Pandora.

Taylor, A. (1993) *Women Drug Users: An Ethnography of a Female Injecting Community.* Oxford: Clarendon.

United Nations (2000) *World Drug Report 2000.* Oxford: Oxford University Press.

Velleman, R. and Orford, J. (1998) *Risk and Resilience: The Children of Problem Drinking Parents Grown Up.* Reading: Harwood.

Velleman, R., Bennett, G., Miller, T., Orford, J., Rigby, K. and Tod, A. (1993) 'The families of problem drug users: the accounts of fifty close relatives.' *Addiction 88,* 1281–9.

Wibberley, C. and Price, J.F. (2000) 'Young people drug use: facts feelings – implications for the normalization debate.' *Drugs: Education, Prevention and Policy 7,* 2, 147–62.

Chapter 5

HIV/AIDS: Challenging Stigma by Association

Liz Walker

HIV/AIDS is highly stigmatised, as are people and objects associated with it. Evidence from communities seriously affected by HIV/AIDS, such as those in Southern Africa, reveals that family members and partners of people living with HIV/AIDS are 'stigmatised by association'. So too are researchers, carers and health and social care professionals who work with families affected by HIV/AIDS; therefore the nature and quality of support, interventions and research with individuals, families and communities living with HIV/AIDS are compromised. The effects of HIV-related stigma are well known, as are the consequences of isolation and exclusion. Yet stigmatisation has also triggered a powerful positive reaction. In this chapter I argue that South African AIDS workers have confronted stigmatisation (and secondary stigmatisation), challenged discriminatory government policy through the courts, and confronted social differences and inequalities reproduced through stigmatisation.

This chapter has four parts. The first is a discussion of the nature of HIV-related stigma in South Africa. The second considers the notion of associative stigma or disadvantage. It looks specifically at the ways in which those who care for people living with HIV/AIDS (PLWHA) experience stigma and discrimination. Here I draw on research conducted with community-based volunteers (carers) in the Limpopo province in the north-east of South Africa.[1] The third part of the chapter looks at responses to the HIV/AIDS epidemic that directly challenge stigma. I argue that AIDS activism has broken (or at least interrupted) the cycle of 'transmitted deprivation'. By locating the struggle for access to health care (in this case anti-retroviral therapy) within a wider human rights and social justice discourse, AIDS activists (and AIDS workers more generally) have challenged the stigmatisation of HIV/AIDS. I suggest that fighting for the rights of PLWHA can be seen to have an associative advantage (rather than disadvantage). And the chapter ends with an exploration of what lessons may be drawn from the South African example of the Treatment Action Campaign (TAC), for confronting HIV/AIDS-related 'associative stigma' in other contexts.

The stigmatisation of HIV/AIDS in South Africa

> Death from AIDS is accompanied by shame... A death from AIDS is full of disappointment. (Focus Group Discussion (FGD), cited in Posel 2004: 9)

Across the world, people living with HIV/AIDS have been stigmatised and subject to discrimination since the epidemic began. In 1987, Jonathan Mann distinguished between three phases of the AIDS epidemic – the first being the epidemic of HIV infection and the second, the epidemic of AIDS itself. The third he described as 'the social, cultural, economic and political reaction to AIDS [which] is as central to the global challenge as AIDS itself' (Mann, 1987 cited in Panos Dossier, 1990). Some 13 years later, stigma was again placed at the top of the list of 'the five most pressing items on [the] agenda for the world community', by Peter Piot, the Executive Director of UNAIDS, at the tenth meeting of the agency's Programme Coordinating Board in 2000 (Parker and Aggleton, 2003: 14). Yet HIV- and AIDS-related stigma and discrimination remain intact.

On the one hand, this points to the pernicious and pervasive form that HIV-related stigma has taken. But it also highlights problems and limitations with the nature of social science research and analysis on stigma generally and disease stigma in particular. Richard Parker and Peter Aggleton (2003) suggest that the emphasis within the social psychology literature has unsurprisingly been on the individual:

> Much work has tended to focus on stereotyping rather than on structural conditions that produce exclusion from social and economic life, and social psychological analyses have often transformed perceived stigmas into marks or attributes of persons. (2003: 14)

Rather than looking at what 'some individuals do to other individuals', they suggest there is more value in a sociological approach which conceptualises stigma and discrimination as social processes which reproduce inequality and social exclusion (2003: 19). In this framework stigma is functional to social control. In the context of HIV/AIDS, stigma exacerbates pre-existing social divisions by stereotyping and blaming marginalised and excluded groups as responsible for the spread of the disease; for example, African women or gay men. For Parker and Aggleton (2003), stigma always leads to discrimination which has the effect of 'reproducing relations of social inequality that are advantageous to the dominant class [thus maintaining] the socio-political status quo' (Deacon, Stepheny and Prosalendis, 2005: 18).

Whilst it is useful to shift our understanding of stigma away from the psychological model of individual blame, it is problematic to suggest that stigma will always foster social inequality. First, as Deacon *et al.* (2005) point out, the HIV/AIDS epidemic will exacerbate social and health inequalities, regardless of stigmatisation. Gilbert and Walker (2002) argue that the epidemic in South Africa has followed the 'path of least resistance', by widening social divisions, for example, between men and women and further entrenching poverty. Second, stigma is not always functional to social control. It may help to challenge the status quo, particularly when it forms a 'springboard for activism' (Deacon *et al.*, 2005: 18). In this chapter, I argue that AIDS activism has successfully undermined HIV-related stigma, encouraging a 'positive identity'. In an effort to draw our attention to the social and cultural construction (and effects) of stigma and discrimination, the 'social control model' arguably places too little attention on individual agency and resistance. Understanding HIV-related stigma (and stigma by association) thus requires an analysis that integrates individual and social levels of explanation. Joffe (1999) provides a useful framework for doing so. She argues that people's responses to danger (in this case HIV/AIDS) draw on universal defence mechanisms called 'splitting' and 'projection' – separating good from bad, and rejecting the bad by projecting it onto the 'other' (Joffe, 1999). Disease stigma is a process whereby people use splitting of the good and the bad to forge protected identities by projecting risk and deviance onto outgroups. 'Stigmatisation thus creates a sense of control and immunity from danger at an individual level because it distances people cognitively and emotionally from risk' (Deacon *et al.*, 2005: 19). The choice of 'outgroup' is shaped by biological, cultural, situational, social and political contexts. Discrimination and the reproduction of social inequality only result when other enabling factors and circumstances exist. According to Joffe (1999), stigma is an emotional response to danger that helps to make people feel safer. She argues that it is not even a conscious process, which explains why it is not easily modified through education. Stigmatisation is thus an individual reaction to perceived or real danger that draws on shared social representations of deviance to distance people from risk (Deacon *et al.*, 2005: 31). In South Africa HIV/AIDS has always been accompanied by secrecy, shame and stigma and it is precisely the conjunction of individual fear, cultural beliefs, the biology of the disease and social inequality that makes HIV/AIDS stigma so profound, yet simultaneously a catalyst for change and social justice.

There has been some high-profile media coverage of HIV-related stigma in South Africa and its consequences, some of which have been extreme. The murder of Gugu Dlamini[2] by a group of people in Kwa-Zulu Natal, after she publicly revealed her HIV positive status, is one example. Although South Africa's high HIV prevalence rates (approximately 20%) are often attributed to stigma and its effects, HIV-related stigma is surprisingly under-researched in South Africa.[3]

Recent research reveals that HIV/AIDS is so stigmatised that in many communities it cannot be named or certainly not in public. Jo Stein (2003: 95) states that in:

> the Western Cape province, HIV/AIDS is called 'ulwazi' which means 'that thing'. This has been taken to suggest that HIV/AIDS is seen, not only as a disease that has no cure, but as one which is so stigmatised, it cannot even be referred to by name.

In a study of AIDS death in a village in the Bushbuckridge district of the South African lowveld, Jonathan Stadler (2003: 127) similarly shows that AIDS was publicly hidden and concealed. He describes a conversation with mourners leaving a funeral:

> At the funeral, a young schoolgirl was being buried. The cause of her death was announced in vague terms. Those who were called to witness her death pronounced that she had been 'sick for a long time'. Not much more was said, but the look on the faces of the many mourners suggested that there was more to it than that. Later, small groups of mourners drifted away from the funeral talking as they made their way home. I asked what had caused the death of such a young woman. One of the men held up four fingers, silently spelling out the phrase 'three numbers plus bonus' – a direct reference to the national lottery that pays out dividends for matching three or more numbers. Here, however, this signalled a coded reference to the initials A-I-D-S.

As part of the wider study of the effects of AIDS death in Agincourt, Posel (2004: 9) highlights similar sentiments when outlining the intensity of AIDS stigma. 'In the emotional register of AIDS in Agincourt...pity, sympathy and compassion seem to have little place. It is the emotions of shame and disgust which are uppermost.' This research reveals that the stigma of AIDS:

> leads families to banish children who are infected with AIDS; husbands chase away wives who have become sick with AIDS; everyday life is

structured by strenuous regimes of public secrecy and disavowal of AIDS; priests are frightened to mention the subject of AIDS at funerals even when (and perhaps especially when) people know the cause of death. (Posel, 2004: 23)

AIDS-related stigma is seen both as the 'mark of bad living' (promiscuous sex) and dehumanising death (Posel, 2004).[4] Fear – of a painful and degrading death, of contamination and contagion – lie at the heart of AIDS stigma, as does the biology of the epidemic, for HIV/AIDS is enigmatic and remains incurable. It is unpredictable, concealable, 'mysterious, elusive, difficult to understand and constantly changing' (Walker, Reid and Cornell, 2004: 100).

Research highlighting the highly stigmatised nature of HIV/AIDS in South Africa is at odds with the findings of a survey conducted in 2002 which found that the majority of South Africans express attitudes of acceptance towards people living with HIV/AIDS; for example, 74 per cent of respondents said they would share a meal with someone who is HIV positive (NMF/HSRC, 2002). Stein (2003), however, rightly points out that researching stigma in this way may be of limited value as few people are likely to reveal stigmatising attitudes publicly. To be seen to be discriminating against people who are HIV positive is no longer socially acceptable (Reid and Walker, 2003). The nature and form of HIV-related stigma in South Africa, particularly in the context of programmes to make antiretroviral therapy more widely available, remains a research priority. Yet, if AIDS stigma is under-researched in South Africa, so too is the stigma that attaches to those associated with HIV/AIDS.

Stigma by association

In *Stigma: Notes on the Management of Spoiled Identity*, Goffman (1963: 43) describes secondary or 'courtesy stigma' as a condition which is experienced by:

> the individual who is related through the social structure to a stigmatised individual – a relationship that leads the wider society to treat both individuals in some respects as one. Thus, the loyal spouse of the mental patient, the daughter of the ex-con, the parent of the cripple, the friend of the blind, the family of the hangman, are all obliged to share some of the discredit of the stigmatised person to whom they are related.

The problems, he says, that are faced by stigmatised persons 'spread out in waves, of diminishing intensity' (Goffman, 1963: 43). 'Courtesy stigma' is often the reason for relations and associations with the stigmatised to be avoided or indeed end. Goffman's (1963) notion of courtesy stigma or stigma by association has been usefully engaged in other contexts to describe an associative disadvantage.

In his work on the experiences of living with a disabled sibling, Peter Burke (2004: 9–12) uses the term 'disability by association' to describe the ways in which one family member's disability can affect the whole family. Siblings and other family members can become isolated because of the impact of disability – by assuming 'undesirable social characteristics' – and may therefore become disadvantaged and experience associative stigma.[5] Burke (2004: 12) argues:

> Living with disability may make a family feel isolated and alone, especially if social encounters reinforce the view that a disabled person is somehow, 'not worthy'... Unfortunately, the feeling of 'image association' in a negative sense will often pervade the whole family, and whatever way they accommodate negative perceptions, such experiences are not restricted to those with disabilities themselves.

Family members, partners of people living with HIV/AIDS, carers and health and social care professionals, as well as AIDS activists, identified groups of people such as gay men, and injecting drug users – even objects associated with HIV/AIDS such as condoms, have been similarly 'stigmatised by association'. Kowalewski (1988) has shown that the:

> stigma associated with HIV is contagious and groups such as gay men are guilty by association and report 'courtesy stigma'; carers and family members may also share the stigma of AIDS and are likewise discredited and suffer enormously as a result of loss of friends and harassment. (Cited in Green, 1995: 558)

Disease stigmatisation associates negatively defined behaviours with people who have specific diseases, 'stacking meanings and values onto biological phenomenon like disease' (Deacon *et al.*, 2005: 23). The reverse can also be true where negatively defined groups can also be seen as disease carriers, for example, African emigrants to the UK are frequently blamed for the increase in HIV. Like Kowalewski, Deacon *et al.* (2005: 24) also point out that once a disease has been stigmatised secondary stigmatisations of related characteristics occur, therefore widening the referential framework for stigma and its potential impact. In the case of HIV/AIDS, courtesy stigma has occurred with tuberculosis (TB), the use of formula feeding and the use of condoms:

> They are used as markers for HIV/AIDS and are therefore stigmatised by association. For example, a school feeding scheme was recently placed in

jeopardy because the cereal was labelled 'AIDS-porridge' due to its use for AIDS patients, and students refused to eat it. (Deacon *et al.*, 2005: 24)

Carers and family members of PLWHA, particularly children,[6] also experience stigma by association, differently and in varying degrees of intensity. Yet, in South Africa, this remains a highly under-researched area and much evidence is indirect and tangential. For example, reference is made to experiences of associative stigma in studies dealing with other issues, such as barriers to treatment, and the negative and humiliating experiences of children whose parents have died of HIV/AIDS, and of older people, particularly women, whose children have died of AIDS-related illnesses. One area of ongoing work that does provide valuable insight into secondary stigmatisation is research with community-based and home-based carers or AIDS volunteers.

In many parts of South Africa community-based care (CBC) and support assists households in caring for people with HIV/AIDS.[7] CBC is defined as:

> all AIDS activities that (1) are based outside conventional health facilities (hospitals, clinics, health centres), but which may have linkages with the formal health and welfare sector and (2) address any aspect of the 'continuum of care and support', from time of infection through to death and impact on survivors. (Russell and Schneider, 2000: 328)

Organisations involved in CBC face a great many challenges; for example, the bulk of services are provided by volunteers whose commitment is often difficult to sustain. And one key barrier to the implementation of CBC is that of stigma. A study of two CBC programmes in Alexandra, north of Johannesburg and Mphophomeni, Kwa-Zulu Natal, revealed that such programmes were stigmatising as households and volunteers became AIDS identified (Stadler, 2001). Volunteers and carers in Mphophomeni 'attempted to allay people's suspicions by promoting themselves as TB treatment observers' (Stadler, 2001: 17). The caregivers often had to disguise the real nature of their visits and their work. 'A volunteer from Alexandra was wary when visiting clients and would quickly change the topic of conversation if anyone came in earshot' (Stadler, 2001: 17). Stadler's study also reveals that volunteers were pressurised by their partners and parents to cease their work because they were also being associated with HIV-infected people and therefore stigmatised.

Interviews with home-based carers in Agincourt also revealed extraordinary levels of HIV-related shame and stigma. Although some carers were allocated to houses in nearby villages by health workers in the clinics, some 'sick houses' were identified through 'informal' means. Villagers and households with sick family members were not willing to identify themselves openly. One commented:

> People help us by whispering that information, because they know the job we are doing. Mostly we dig up information from people who help us uncover people who are hidden in their houses. (Female AIDS carer, Lilydale A Clinic, p.4)

Interviewees stated that the silence and secrecy surrounding the families and households with AIDS was strenuously maintained by the families themselves, fearing associative stigma and discrimination:

> You know the family is highly affected in a sense that the members feel deserted and rejected; they do not feel accepted by the community; they know they will become the laughing stock. They feel as if they have lost their dignity because people tend to think that if a member of the family is dying of AIDS all the members are infected too because they are caring for him and they live with him. If a member of the family is suffering from AIDS, it means they [the rest of the family] are AIDS sufferers too. (Female AIDS carer, Lilydale A Clinic, p.8)

> The community was not accepting that family anymore because they were always talking that she's got AIDS and will pass it on to them and their children. The community hated them. The younger sister of the [person I was caring for] came to see me crying and saying people hated them. She further said her boyfriend deserted her because there is an AIDS sufferer at her home and she must never ever talk to him again because she'll pass AIDS on to him. It means that they all have AIDS because there is an AIDS sufferer at her home. (Female AIDS carer, Interview 2, p.9)

As carers, they also experience ridicule:

> [People] sometimes tease us; they call us government; some call us AIDS. They refer to us as AIDS. (Female AIDS carer, Lilydale A Clinic, p.7)

So severe are the experiences of shame and stigma that people dying of HIV/AIDS could not reveal or name their illness to their carer who is often responsible for much of the person's physical care. One commented:

> Well I can say that we do not know whether a person is suffering from AIDS or other illnesses because surely the clinic sister does not tell what a person is suffering from. Most people think they are dying from TB whereas it is AIDS. For those who know their patients are suffering from AIDS do not tell anyone; they hide; they do not talk about AIDS. (Female AIDS carer, Lilydale A Clinic, p.8)

Another AIDS volunteer said:

> We talk to them and they say they don't know what the matter is with them. You will only be told that he or she has TB. You can't say that [they have AIDS] because they will have a different look towards you. What they know is that you came here because of TB and nothing more. No one ever told us the real problem. Those who I visit don't tell me. (Female AIDS carer, Kildare Clinic, p.6)

These interviews with home-based carers reveal widespread stigmatisation and denial of HIV/AIDS even in the midst of death and family devastation. Distant association with people dying of HIV/AIDS is shaming and stigmatising. In this context the challenges that family members and carers face are immense. Mourning is overshadowed by fear and public conspiracies (in which carers often have to participate) continue to reinforce rather than weaken AIDS-related stigma and discrimination, for there is little doubt that denial and silence accentuates HIV-related stigma.

HIV/AIDS in South Africa has been produced as a site of secrecy, silence and denial. Yet AIDS and its effects are seen and felt everywhere. Over the past ten years government departments, non-governmental organisations (NGOs) and churches have focused on public health prevention programmes such as massive AIDS awareness campaigns, sex education in schools,[8] and widespread distribution of condoms. Matters of sex and sexuality have been in the public domain as never before. Newspaper articles, billboards and radio and television advertisements give both veiled and explicit sexual information, which has extended beyond the AIDS epidemic to generating public discussion of other sexual health problems (Walker *et al.*, 2004: 115).

Research that measures HIV/AIDS knowledge and awareness reports very high levels of understanding, yet prevalence rates continue to rise:

> The paradox of knowledge and denial is seen in the young man who, despite a high level of awareness about HIV, nevertheless acts in a way that puts him at high risk. Nowhere is this paradox more striking than in the juxtaposition of high HIV prevalence and extraordinary levels of AIDS denialism at the highest level of government. (Reid and Walker, 2003: 86)

Denial, fear, stigmatisation sit alongside widespread public knowledge and comprehension. In stark contrast to practices of denial and secrecy, a guiding premise of health and social care professionals, NGOs, AIDS volunteers and AIDS activist groups globally and in South Africa has been an insistence on 'breaking of silences, the naming of secrets, and making public claims to reduce what otherwise has been cast as private shame' (Reid and

Walker, 2003: 86). In the next part of the chapter I look at the way in which South African AIDS activism, in particular, has challenged HIV-related stigma, discrimination and disadvantage and promoted positive 'associative advantage'.

Challenging stigma: Advancing associative advantage

Overcoming AIDS stigma and discrimination has taken many forms. In the Southern African region human rights activists have tried to ensure that laws do not discriminate against people who are HIV positive; for example, in the workplace, in securing life insurance, access to housing, finance and so on. Indeed globally:

> legal protections for people living with HIV/AIDS together with appropriate reporting and enforcement mechanisms (ranging from legal aid services to hotlines for reporting acts of discrimination and violence against people with HIV/AIDS, gay men, women suffering domestic violence and so on), have provided powerful and rapid means of mitigating the worst effects of unequal power relations, social inequality and exclusion that lie at the heart of processes of HIV and AIDS related stigmatisation and discrimination. (Parker and Aggleton, 2003: 22)

But the impact of the law and legal remedies are often limited. Many people face prejudice in spite of the law, which cannot protect them from finger pointing, hostility and social ostracism (Walker et al., 2004). South Africa's constitution is widely regarded as the most progressive in the world, yet millions of people have been denied their 'right to life' because life-prolonging treatment has not, until recently, been made widely available.[9] The legal and constitutional framework is an essential component of an enabling environment in which the rights of PLWHA can be promoted but good laws and policies do not guarantee non-discrimination.

HIV/AIDS education, prevention and intervention programmes have focused on HIV-related stigma, for example, public health campaigns, waged by health and social care professionals, which explode myths about modes of HIV transmission. But Parker and Aggleton (2003) are right to point to limitations of many such programmes because they are designed around models of individual level interventions and not around issues of power, inequality and social exclusion:

> Intervention designs seem to have functioned in large part according to what Freire (1970) long ago identified as a 'banking' theory of pedagogy in which the perceived deficit accounts of those being 'educated' are somehow 'filled' by intervention specialists who presume they know the truth about what is needed. (2003: 21)

These concerns are compounded in an African context where many such interventions have been modelled on Western interpretations and experiences of the epidemic.[10]

Community mobilisation, advocacy and social change, where the voices of stigmatised populations and communities are central, need to be part of multi-agency programmes of intervention aimed at resisting HIV/AIDS-related stigma (Parker and Aggleton 2003). Drawing on Castells' (1997) notion of resistance and project identities Parker and Aggleton (2003: 19) argue that stigmatisation can be resisted in this way. Resistance identities are:

> generated by those actors that are in positions/conditions devalued and/or stigmatised by the logic of domination [or dominant institutions] and project identities are formed when social actors, on the basis of whatever cultural materials are available to them, build a new identity that redefines their position in society, and by so doing, seek the transformation of overall social structure.

It is arguable that civil society's response to HIV/AIDS in South Africa, in particular, the development of the Treatment Action Campaign (TAC) in December 1998, certainly reflects powerful and effective community mobilisation and indeed a resistance identity.

Civil society's response to HIV/AIDS in South Africa has a strong human rights element. Struggles around HIV/AIDS in South Africa have been waged on many fronts and by many different groups, including social workers located in educational and community settings, and health workers engaged in the prevention, treatment and clinical research on HIV/AIDS. Yet social and community activism around HIV/AIDS, particularly that of the TAC, has profoundly influenced the course of the epidemic in South Africa and shaped the work of many health and social care professionals. Some forms of social activism in South Africa can be traced back to community activism in Western countries, particularly the actions of human rights groups in the United States. Groups such as ACT-UP (AIDS Coalition to Unleash Power) started a dialogue between civil society, the pharmaceutical industry and medical regulatory authorities, when it won the right to fast-track treatment while drug trials were still in progress. This form of political action clearly influenced South African responses to the epidemic (Walker *et al.*, 2004). At the outset, much of the TAC's work was directed at pharmaceutical companies. 'The TAC's initial focus was on raising awareness among people with HIV of treatments, campaigning for lower medicine prices, and advocating for the right to treatment using antiretroviral drugs' (Heywood, 2004: 98). But the TAC also drew on a strong tradition of political activism in South Africa – the struggle for political equality and social justice embodied in the anti-apartheid movement. The TAC began to emerge as a community-based response to HIV, projecting the voice of PLWHA, the vast majority of whom could not afford medical treatment.[11] The TAC did not anticipate that the most vociferous opponent of their 'access to treatment campaign' would, ironically, be the South African government, particularly President Thabo Mbeki. Over the past five years, the TAC has waged legal and civil battles with the government to ensure that Highly Active Anti-Retroviral Therapy (HAART) is made available to PLWHA through the state health sector, winning global recognition and support for their work and establishing themselves as one of the most significant health and social movements in South Africa.[12]

The 'access to treatment' campaign was supplemented by a campaign of 'openness and acceptance'. Heywood[13] (2004: 100) argues:

> for a community-based AIDS activist movement to emerge and successfully demand access to treatment it was necessary for it also to confront the multi-layered problems of stigma and denial that exist first and foremost in communities.

Tackling stigma was therefore central to the TAC's treatment campaign and they deployed a number of strategies to do so. One of the most powerful has been the 'simple device' of the HIV-positive T-shirt:

> [It] proved to have remarkable power in confronting people's attitudes about HIV at the same time as emerging as a badge of the activist community and signifying both solidarity between the living and tribute to those who have died. (Heywood, 2004: 100)

Seale (2004: 17–18) comments:

> the HIV-positive t-shirts worn by TAC members and TAC supporters (most famously by Nelson Mandela) are a symbolic gesture of challenging stigma by taking power away from those who could, left unchallenged, be in a position to stigmatise. Labelling yourself before you can be labelled by others is a tried and tested tactic that has been used by minority groups throughout history and works because it takes power and ammunition away from the 'powerful'.

Thousands of people (HIV positive and negative) associated themselves with the TAC and in this way established a positive collective identity. Associating with the human rights campaign for 'access to treatment' necessarily meant associating with HIV and its embedded stigma. Yet this was a positive association with a stigmatised condition that brought with it an associative advantage. Confronting HIV/AIDS-related stigma was firmly located within the framework of social justice and human rights. In the context of the TAC, PLWHA, HIV negative people and social advocates generally, lawyers, health and social care professionals became social activists effectively lobbying against stigma and for 'the right to life'. Parker and Aggleton (2003) argue that it is precisely through fostering an activist identity, based on the assertion that PLWHA are being denied fundamental human rights, that the range and effects of HIV/AIDS stigma and its associative effects can be reduced.

Learning from the South African experience

Exploring the issue of HIV-related 'associative stigma' through the lens of the TAC in particular, and the experience of HIV/AIDS stigma in South Africa more generally, is instructive for AIDS activists, and health and social care professionals working in other contexts and countries for it highlights a number of key lessons for research and practice. HIV-related stigma is a global challenge. In this chapter I have written about the South African experience of confronting HIV/AIDS stigma (and secondary stigma), yet the task of understanding, researching and intervening to combat HIV-related stigma and discrimination is a universal and recurrent one requiring innovative responses.

The example of the TAC points to the value of reconceptualising stigma in a way that highlights HIV/AIDS stigma as a social phenomenon that changes over time. If HIV/AIDS-related stigma is also conceived as a matter of social inequality, social exclusion and social justice then the possibilities for challenging stigma extend beyond the more traditional focus on behaviour change and individual intervention:

> The time is ripe to build upon existing empirical evidence, as well as the literature on community organising and community building...to begin developing new models for advocacy and social change in response to HIV and AIDS-related stigmatisation and discrimination. (Parker and Aggleton, 2003: 21)

This is particularly important in the context of other associated and compounding experiences of prejudice and discrimination. For example, African people with HIV/AIDS who have migrated to the UK face HIV-related stigma but also racism and xenophobia and are blamed for growing rates of HIV infection more generally.[14]

In this chapter, I have shown that the TAC utilised a wide range of approaches to advance their campaign for free and universal access to treatment for PLWHA. They invoked successful legal strategies, focused on the prevention of HIV infection through education and not just on access to treatment: their strategies and policies were multi-layered and involved a multi-agency approach. But arguably, their publicness is one of their most important strategies. Public disclosure and a public HIV/AIDS presence have been at the centre of their efforts to destigmatise HIV/AIDS in South Africa. Taking HIV/AIDS out of clinics and hospitals, moving it away from offices and private spaces and into the community, domesticating and normalising it, makes it part of society more generally. And, the destigmatising power of high-profile public figures disclosing their HIV positive status cannot be underestimated. Making AIDS public will mean that 'we can care openly and without the constraints that silence and stigma currently impose' (Preston-Whyte, 2003: 94).

It is PLWHA that have been the backbone of the TAC in South Africa. Indeed, the people most affected by the epidemic, the people most in need of treatment and support, should lead efforts to campaign for their rights, to challenge stigma and disadvantage. Yet they should not carry the burden alone and of course, 'intervention would be most effective if HIV-negative people joined the PLWHA as activists [and social advocates] against stigma' (Deacon et al., 2005: 79).

Confronting HIV/AIDS-related stigma is also not simply a question of remedying ignorance, myths and misconceptions by providing medically correct information. It is fundamentally about confronting fear and prejudice. Earlier in the chapter, I argued that 'stigma could be seen as an emotional response to danger that helps people to feel safer – [that] it is not a rational or even conscious process' (Deacon et al., 2005: 80). This explains why it is not easily challenged or changed by education. Deacon et al. (2005: 80) suggest that the most effective educational interventions taking local contexts and meanings associated with HIV/AIDS into account are community-based, and are linked to skills-building, counselling and social interaction programmes. Educational intervention needs to teach people that stigma is a 'social problem and not a problem of individual ignorance' (Deacon et al., 2005: 81). Social prejudice, social exclusion and disease need to be clearly linked and openly discussed. Deacon et al. (2005) suggest that using historical examples of people with other diseases that are no longer a threat to the community, such as leprosy, can be a useful way of demonstrating the social nature of stigmatisation.

In South Africa, the Treatment Action Campaign has grown into a powerful social and health movement, creating a culture of challenge, which has gone a long way to creating a positive association with a stigmatised condition, making it an example of resilience and empowerment. Such widespread community action and engagement may not be appropriate in other contexts but it demonstrates the value and power of understanding disease stigma as a social concern which requires a social response as much if not more as a health response. This means that health and social care professionals may need to work in new and innovative ways. Health professionals can and do make a powerful contribution to the lives of PLWHA but health can also remove HIV/AIDS from its social context by not making wider connections particularly around questions of stigma and stigma by association. It is a significant challenge to tackle disease stigma and disadvantage and not just disease. This is a challenge that equally confronts social care professionals, including social workers. Holloway (2005) suggests that 'it is at the heart of social work to challenge oppression and injustice, to seek to alleviate suffering and hardship': in short to promote social change and social justice. She argues that social work has in recent years lost sight of its 'moral agenda'. Confronting HIV/AIDS-related stigma and secondary associative stigma provides an opportunity to highlight an under-researched area of enquiry and interrupt the cycle of transmitted disadvantage.

Notes

1   These interviews form part of a collaborative study of life and death in Agincourt, a deep rural area in which rates of AIDS-related death have increased significantly over the past few years. The research is collaboration between the School of Public Health, University of the Witwatersrand, and the Wits Institute of Social and Economic Research (WISER), where I am research associate and an investigator in the research team. 'The broad aim of the research is to examine how people in Agincourt make sense of, and react to, rampant illness and "bad death", and to assess its impact on their perceptions of, and aspirations for, life. The study is designed as a triangulation of qualitative and quantitative methods of inquiry, in a two phase process of research' (Posel, 2004: 1). The interviews with community-based volunteers were conducted in the first phase of the research along with six other key informant interviews and 48 focus groups.

2   The TAC's first HIV-positive T-shirt carried the picture of Gugu Dlamini, who was an active member of the National Association of People with AIDS, and the slogan 'never again'.

3   It is researched indirectly through other studies. See for example, Etibet *et al.* (2004), Mundell, Gcabo and Visser (2004) and Visser (2004).

4   See Sontag (1991) for a discussion on 'bad death'.

5   For a discussion on stigmatisation of families of individuals with mental health problems, see Angermeyer and Matschinger (2003).

6   Writing about fosterage patterns in the context of AIDS, Madhavan (2004: 1451) demonstrates that children orphaned by AIDS are severely stigmatised and are

often shunned by their relatives. It is estimated that in South Africa four million children will be orphaned by 2015 (Whiteside and Sunter, 2000). For a recent study on the needs of children of HIV-positive parents/carers in Scotland see Kay *et al.* (2004).

7 There are many similar projects throughout other parts of Southern Africa such as Family AIDS Caring Trust (FACT) in Zimbabwe, the Catholic Diocese in Zambia's copperbelt and the AIDS Support Organisation (TASO) in Uganda (Madhavan, 2004; Russell and Schneider, 2000). Drug adherence required with the treatment of TB has been successfully monitored in many parts of Africa using the DOTS (Directly Observable Treatment System).

8 For a discussion of a recent social work intervention among South African school children see Sewpaul and Raniga (2005).

9 Despite the fact that the South African government is making provision for the roll out of anti-retroviral treatment, access is still very uneven and slow in forthcoming in many areas.

10 Heald (2002) points to the failure of HIV/AIDS intervention programmes in Botswana, because they were based on Western and therefore biomedical models of explanation and intervention. 'The language of AIDS is the language of Western science and policy. All programmes in Africa, whether medical or social, have been dominated by the WHO, and more recently UNAIDS, as well as USAID and other Western-based NGOs' (2002: 1).

11 Addressing the impact of poverty, affordability and access to treatment for HIV/AIDS, Mr Justice Edwin Cameron, speaking at the 13th International AIDS Conference in Durban, said, 'I speak of the gap between rich and poor, not as an observer or as a commentator, but with intimate personal knowledge. I am an African. I am living with AIDS. I therefore count as one among the forbidding statistics of AIDS in Africa. Amid the poverty of Africa, I stand before you because I am able to purchase health and vigour. I am here because I can pay for life itself.'

12 For a detailed discussion of the TAC's campaign for access to HAART see Heywood (2004).

13 Mark Heywood has been a member of the TAC executive committee since its inception.

14 For an overview of recent research on HIV stigma and discrimination among African migrants to the UK see Keogh (2004); also Weston (2003) and Doyle and Anderson (2005) for a discussion on marginalised communities and HIV/AIDS in London.

References

Angermeyer, M.C. and Matschinger, H. (2003) 'The stigma of mental illness: effects of labeling on public attitudes towards people with mental disorder.' *Acta Psychiatrica Scandinavica 108*, 4, 304–9.

Burke, P. (2004) *Brothers and Sisters of Disabled Children.* London: Jessica Kingsley Publishers.

Castells, M. (1997) *The Power of Identity.* Oxford: Blackwell.

Deacon, H., Stepheny, I. and Prosalendis, S. (2005) *Understanding HIV/AIDS Stigma.* Pretoria: HSRC Press.

Doyle, L. and Anderson, J. (2005) '"My fear is to fall in love again…" How HIV-positive African women survive in London.' *Social Science and Medicine 60,* 1729–38.

Etibet, M.A., Fransman, D., Forsyth, B., Coetzee, N. and Hussey, G. (2004) 'Integrating prevention of mother to child HIV transmission into antenatal care: learning from experiences of women in South Africa.' *AIDS Care 16,* 1, 37–46.

Gilbert, L. and Walker, L (2002) 'Treading the path of least resistance: social inequality and HIV/AIDS in South Africa.' *Social Science and Medicine 54,* 1093–1110.

Goffman, E. (1963) *Stigma. Notes on the Management of Spoiled Identity.* London: Penguin.

Green, G. (1995) 'Attitudes towards people with HIV: are they as stigmatising as people with HIV perceive them to be?' *Social Science and Medicine 41,* 4, 557–68.

Heald, S. (2002) 'It's never as easy as ABC: understandings of AIDS in Botswana.' *African Journal of AIDS Research 1,* 1, 1–10.

Heywood, M. (2004) 'The price of denial.' *Development Update 5,* 3, 93–122.

Holloway, M. (2005) Editorial. *British Journal of Social Work 35,* 303–304.

HSRC (2002) *Nelson Mandela/HSRC Study of HDS: South African National HIV Prevalence, Behaviour Risks and Mass Media Household Survey 2002.* Pretoria: HSRC Press.

Joffe, H. (1999) *Risk and 'The Other'.* Cambridge: Cambridge University Press.

Kay, E., Tisdall, H.K., Cree, V and Wallace, J. (2004) 'Children in need? Listening to children whose parent or carer is HIV positive.' *British Journal of Social Work 34,* 1097–1113.

Keogh, P. (2004) 'Outsider status.' *Impact 9,* 7–11.

Madhavan, S. (2004) 'Fosterage patterns in the age of AIDS: continuity and change.' *Social Science and Medicine 58,* 1443–54.

Mann, J. (1987) Statement at an Informal Briefing on AIDS to the 42nd Session of the United Nations General Assembly, 20 October.

Mundell, J., Gcabo, R. and Visser, M. (2004) 'A Review of Interventions to Reduce Stigma in South Africa: What have we Learnt?' Paper presented at the SAHARA Conference, Cape Town, 9–12 May.

Panos Dossier (1990) *The 3rd Epidemic. Repercussions of the Fear of AIDS.* London: The Panos Institute.

Parker, R. and Aggleton, P. (2003) 'HIV and AIDS-related stigma and discrimination: a conceptual framework and implications for action.' *Social Science and Medicine 57,* 13–24.

Posel, D. (2004) 'Sex, Death and Embodiment: Reflections on Stigma of AIDS in Agincourt, South Africa.' Paper presented at the symposium on Life and Death in a Time of AIDS: The Southern African Experience, WISER 14–16 October 2004.

Preston-Whyte, E.M. (2003) 'Contexts of vulnerability: sex, secrecy and HIV/AIDS.' *African Journal of AIDS Research 2,* 2, 89–94.

Reid, G. and Walker, L. (2003) 'Secrecy, stigma and HIV/AIDS.' *African Journal of AIDS Research 2,* 2, 85–8.

Russell, M. and Schneider, H. (2000) 'Models of Community-Based HIV/AIDS Care and Support.' *South African Health Review 2000.* Durban: Health Systems Trust.

Seale, A. (2004) 'Breaking a vicious cycle that threatens the global response to AIDS.' *Impact 9,* 15–18.

Sewpaul, V. and Raniga, T. (2005) 'Producing Results: Researching Social Work Interventions on HIV/AIDS in the Context of the School.' In R. Adams, L. Dominelli and M. Payne (eds) *Social Work Futures. Crossing Boundaries, Transforming Practice.* Basingstoke: Palgrave Macmillan.

Sontag, S. (1991) *Illness as Metaphor and AIDS and Its Metaphors.* London: Penguin.

Stadler, J. (2001) '"He has a Heart of Listening": Reflections on a Community-Based Care and Support Programme for People Infected with HIV/AIDS.' Paper presented to the AIDS in Context Conference, University of the Witwatersrand, 4–7 April.

Stadler, J. (2003) 'The young, the rich and the beautiful: secrecy, suspicion and discourses of AIDS in the South African Lowveld.' *African Journal of AIDS Research 2*, 2, 127–40.

Stein, J. (2003) 'HIV/AIDS stigma: the latest dirty secret.' *African Journal of AIDS Research 2*, 2, 95–101.

Visser, M. (2004) 'HIV+ Women's Experiences of Stigma and Social Support.' Paper presented at the SAHARA Conference, Cape Town, 9–12 May.

Walker, L., Reid, G. and Cornell, M. (2004) *Waiting to Happen: HIV/AIDS in South Africa.* Cape Town: Double Storey.

Weston, H.J. (2003) 'Public honour, private shame and HIV: issues affecting sexual health service delivery in London's South Asian communities.' *Health and Place 9*, 109–17.

Whiteside, A. and Sunter, C. (2000) *AIDS: The Challenge for South Africa.* Cape Town: Human and Rousseau Tafelberg.

Chapter 6

Ageing against the Grain: Gay Men and Lesbians

Elizabeth Price

A generally negative approach towards ageing in Western societies has resulted in the fact that, in general, older people tend to be perceived as either asexual or celibate. These ageist assumptions tend, in turn, to be coupled with implicit presumptions of heterosexuality – few studies of ageing in the general population have addressed issues of sexual orientation despite a conservative estimate which suggests there are currently between 545,000 and 872,000 gay men and lesbians over the age of 65 in the UK (Wellings *et al.*, 1994).

Empirical studies highlighting the specific experience of older gay men and lesbians in the UK are, therefore, exceptional (see, for example, Heaphy, Yip and Thompson, 2003; Kitchen, 2003; Opening Doors in Thanet, 2003), though the relatively recent interest of a small number of researchers means that they are becoming more numerous. Nonetheless, older gay and lesbian people remain, to a large degree, an invisible constituent of social, political and academic life in twenty-first-century society.

This chapter charts the modest rise in interest in gay and lesbian ageing and identity, from the first tentative, primarily North American, studies in the 1980s to more contemporary work which includes studies originating in the UK. The intention here is to explore this work into the lives of older gay men and lesbians and to highlight and explore the intersections around the stereotypes and associated stigma related to ageing in a non-heterosexual context.

A note on terminology

Given a history of pathologisation and oppression, gay men and lesbian women are understandably exquisitely sensitive to the significance and nuance of language. As such, the word 'homosexual' is rejected here as a medically crafted, homogeneous, term with explicit overtones of early sexology. Similarly rejected is the ubiquitous 'gay community', as lesbian women may object to its indisputably male bias – gay men and lesbian women are thus the terms used here as language that is widely used and accepted by gay and lesbian people.

In terms of omission, it is currently in vogue, when discussing matters relating to sexual minority communities, to employ the acronym LGBT (lesbian, gay, bisexual and transgender), occasionally extended to include intersex people (I) and those who identify as queer (Q). The resulting somewhat unwieldy acronym is attractive in terms of its undeniable inclusivity and there is no intention here to purposefully exclude any sexual minority. In tandem with Wilton (2000: xviii), however, it is felt that issues of bisexuality deserve distinct and separate attention and that 'an identity constructed around deeply felt unhappiness with one's biological sex is different in kind from one constructed around same-sex desire'.

A history of sexual stigma

There is much debate concerning the history, not only of homosexuality but also, more important, the social category 'the homosexual'. There is tacit agreement, however, that whilst same-sex relations have occurred throughout history, the social category of 'the homosexual' is a construct positioned firmly in the late nineteenth century – a creation, in effect, of 'definition and self-definition' (Weeks, 1985: 6).

In the nineteenth century science and medicine skilfully constructed 'the homosexual' as a *type* of person rather than a person who chose to take part in specific sexual practices. The word 'homosexual' thus came to refer to something someone *was* rather than something someone *did* (Carr, 2005: 171). As Foucault famously stated, the nineteenth-century homosexual became:

> personage, a past, a case history and a childhood, in addition to being a type of life, a life form and a morphology...nothing that went into his total composition was unaffected by his sexuality. It was everywhere present in him: at the root of all his actions because it was their insidious and indefinitely active principle...it was consubstantial with him, less a habitual sin than a singular nature. (Foucault, 1990: 43)

Unsurprisingly, the social construction of homosexuality, in conjunction with other perceived sexual aberrations, led to a variety of largely negative perceptions and stereotypes.

As a result, early twenty-first-century sexual politics, characterised by superficially tolerant attitudes to sexual minorities, referred to by Kehoe (1989: 53) as 'the social pendulum swing towards liberalism', effectively mask the fact that the cohort of gay and lesbian people now approaching old age have, of necessity, developed their sexual personae through and by a variety of socially constructed incarnations of homosexuality.

Gay men and lesbians have been perceived as deviant, weak, perverted, sinners, illegal, a public menace, the unfortunate victims of arrested development and, perhaps most tellingly, in the case of psychiatry, a suitable case for treatment (Kochman, 1997: 2) – an encyclopaedia of negativity referred to by Heaphy (2005: 133) as a 'hegemonic stigmatising discourse'. Unsurprisingly, the most readily available identity for gay men and lesbians before the late 1960s and the 'nascent reformulation and representation of homosexuality' (Rosenfeld, 2003: 1) brought about by the Stonewall uprising was a largely negative and wholly stigmatised one.

Stigma has, therefore, become 'a conceptual keystone of homosexual identity' (Rosenfeld, 2003: 10) and this stigma and its close associate, oppression, have become centrally implicated in the lived experience of older lesbian women and gay men (Langley, 2001). Indeed, a number of studies have shown that older gay and lesbian people themselves describe the period in which they grew up as largely hostile towards their sexuality (Adelman, 1991; Kimmel and Sang, 1995). Stigma, oppression and fear do not combine to create a favourable environment in which to identify with a sexual minority and many older gay and lesbian people may have spent a lifetime concealing their sexual orientation from family, friends and employers, perhaps feeling forced to maintain superficially heteronormative lifestyles. Sex between men was, until 1967, a criminal offence (a situation unchanged in Scotland until 1980), and many gay men lived the most important aspects of their lives largely concealed from society or, alternatively, maintained heterosexual relationships believing these to be normal and, above all, expected (Pugh, 2002; Seidman, 2004).

For lesbians, the situation was little better for, though their sexual preferences were not actually illegal, having been notoriously invalidated by Queen Victoria when she questioned the existence of lesbians in discussion over the Labouchere Amendment to the Criminal Assessment Act, in 1885 (Manthorpe and Price, 2006), they too were forced to lead secretive and largely unacknowledged lives, as one of Kehoe's (1989) respondents illustrates:

> I have no regrets about my life long designation as a lesbian, but did experience years of unhappiness when I had to live in the closet because of it

and forced myself to pretend to heterosexuality in my social and sexual relationships when within me, emotionally and physically, none existed. That is one of the cruelties of the homosexual's lot in our society, and it represents to me all those miserable years which now in my old age can no longer hurt me – now that it is too late to matter. (Kehoe, 1989: 22)

Gay men and lesbian women in the 1940s and 1950s, who may have lived life within the confines of the closet rather than embrace a stigmatised identity, may have felt it necessary to downplay their true sexual identity. This may have resulted in their true sexual selves appearing to be either non-existent or only a minor constituent of their psychological make-up. Indeed, for some people, the 'sheer magnitude of energy and focus' spent managing their stigmatised identity in order to avoid suspicion and exposure sometimes shaped a whole way of life and the closet proved to be a rational social and cultural location for gay men and lesbians and, for many, it became a 'way to accommodate being the bearer of a polluted identity but at a considerable psychic and social cost' (Seidman, 2004: 10–39).

Given the information outlined above, it is not surprising to note that the most readily available sexual identity for gay men and lesbians in the first part of the last century was one based on negativity, fear and shame. Many people grew up in a society that promulgated homosexuality as:

> something awful, like a horribly contagious disease or some unimaginable perversion. In their families, schools, and churches, they were taught that there is only one normal, right, and good sexuality: heterosexuality. (Seidman, 2004: 123)

This period, pre-Stonewall, is referred to by Rosenfeld (2003) as one in which gay men and lesbians were forced to internalise a 'discreditable' identity, a notion she contrasts with post-Stonewall and post-gay and -lesbian liberation generations who, she suggests, were able to internalise an 'accreditable' identity. She asserts that older gay men and lesbians fall, by default, into one or other identity cohort and that it is this arbitrary chronological accident that is likely to determine, to a large degree, their sense of personal and social identity.

The notion of identity cohorts appears to be a popular one in gay and lesbian research. Cohler (1999) proffers a similar concept suggesting that gay men and lesbians might be perceived as growing up in one of four distinct generations, the pre-Stonewall generation, the Stonewall generation, the post-Stonewall generation and the generation coming of age at the turn of the century (cited in Cahill, South and Spade, 2000).

Those lucky enough to fall into the cohorts post-Stonewall may, as Rosenfeld (2003) suggests, have benefited from the liberationist and feminist movements that proliferated in the late 1960s and early 1970s. These movements, she argues, effectively 'changed the symbolic and practical terrain on which gay men and women negotiated their past and present lives' (2003: 3). There were, however, many gay men and lesbians who had lived through the preceding period and who, despite the efforts of liberationists, were left with a legacy of fear and shame having confronted, first hand, a period in the history of sexuality in which the public gaze was anything but benevolent.

Nonetheless, this cohort of gay men and lesbians aged during a period when public and political perceptions of homosexuality began, at least on a superficial level, to alter. However, far from feeling more at ease with a sexual identity that demanded more prominent public space, they were forced to face a new set of pejorative images that linked, in a largely negative manner, the process of ageing with a non-heterosexual identity.

Images of gay and lesbian ageing

For many older gay men and lesbians, pejorative stereotypes abounded. These depicted older gay men as becoming increasingly effeminate with age, alienated from friends and family, shunned by the gay community and forced to prey on young children and pursue anonymous sexual contacts in public places.

Older lesbians, when their existence was recognised at all, were similarly depicted as heartless, childless, unemotional and mannish-looking, again, attempting, in desperation, to seduce younger women until bitter and defeated, without the support of family or friends, they live alone until death (Berger, 1982: 237; Deevey, 1990: 35). Kehoe (1989) noted that there were fewer stereotypes relating to older lesbian woman than men, something she put down to women's greater general invisibility and suggested that this also reflected their triply disregarded social standing being female, aged and deviant. If they were considered at all, Kehoe (1989: 64) stated, it was as 'pathetic, freakish figures, rejected by their families and hiding out of shame'.

It was left to a small number of researchers in the gay and lesbian community, primarily in North America, to challenge some of these stereotypical images of the older gay man and lesbian and to illustrate the realities of ageing in a non-heterosexual context. This research was the first in a growing body of work that successfully challenged the negative images and stereotypes relating to gay and lesbian ageing.

Berger (1982) was perhaps the first, and certainly the most widely cited, researcher to explore the lives of older gay men. He surveyed 112 and

interviewed 10 gay men between the ages of 40 and 79; in so doing, he successfully challenged many of the pejorative stereotypes that both general
society and the gay community itself held about them – though it should be
stressed that Berger's working definition of old age was anyone over the age
of 40, a point which highlights one of the criticisms regularly aired towards
gay and, to a lesser extent, lesbian communities – that ageism appears to be
functioning more overtly than in wider society.

The stereotypes Berger (1982) set out to challenge, whilst insidious and
undoubtedly powerful, have been successfully discredited by the early
research referred to here and more recent work, which has consistently
demonstrated that older gay men and lesbians are generally psychologically
healthy and have high levels of self-acceptance. Moreover, they have the
ability to successfully manage the 'coming out' process, and the resulting
stigmatised identity 'that was in disfavour almost everywhere' has also
ensured that the ageing gay man or lesbian woman faces the stigma attached
to old age with a well-prepared set of psychological defences (Berger, 1982,
1996; Cahill *et al.*, 2000; Deevey, 1990; Dorfman *et al.*, 1995; Heaphy *et al.*,
2003; Kimmel, 1978; Quam and Whitford, 1992; Turnbull, 2001).

Another reason why homosexual people age more successfully, Berger
(1982) suggested, is the differing way in which homosexual and heterosexual people experience and manage role loss in later life. The role losses
experienced by heterosexuals, such as those related to children leaving
home or those associated with retirement and death – the loss of the role of
spouse or active provider – are, he stated, often absent for the gay or lesbian
person who is less likely to have children or, by virtue of the same-sex relationship, is less likely to be 'subjected to male–female discrepancy in life
expectancy', thus being 'less likely to outlive a partner for many years as is
common among heterosexual widows' (Berger, 1982: 238). Similarly,
Friend (1980) suggested that the adoption of flexible gender roles throughout the life span may have allowed the gay man or lesbian to develop high
levels of independence and a positive self-image which, in turn, positively
influences their adjustment to the ageing process. From a lesbian perspective, this point is mirrored by Healey (1994) who notes that, throughout
their lifetimes, many lesbians have placed a high premium on their independence and self-reliance. They have developed, in the process, 'special
and sophisticated strategies' to enable them to survive and a number of skills
which heterosexual women are more likely to assign to men (Healey, 1994:
110–113).

Furthermore, the pressures to conform to gendered expectations of
physical attractiveness are, perhaps, less pronounced than for heterosexual
women. Older lesbians may thus be able to manage the physical signs of

ageing more positively than heterosexual women (Laner, 1997). Laner's (1997) contention is given credence by more recent British research in which a number of female participants suggested 'the privileging of youth was less of an issue in lesbian communities that it was for women in mainstream cultures' (Heaphy *et al.*, 2003: 7). This perhaps brings into question the notion that the lesbian community, in tandem with the gay male community, is wholly preoccupied with maintaining youthfulness and striving for physical perfection. In contrast, however, Heaphy *et al.* (2003: 8) noted that their male respondents perceived that being gay made them more conscious of the ageing process which, the authors note, 'points to significant gender differences in the meanings lesbians and gay men attached to ageing'.

Successful ageing may be directly related to the strength of individuals' support systems throughout the lifespan and, whilst the support systems that older gay men and lesbians have relied upon showed, according to Dorfman *et al.* (1995), little difference to those of the general population, in terms of the levels or sources of support used it has been found, perhaps unsurprisingly, that gay men and lesbians generally have less support from families of origin but more from friends. This conclusion is underlined by recent work which has shown that the value placed by older gay men and lesbians on friendship – the 'family of choice'– as opposed to biological family ties is significant (Donovan, Heaphy and Weeks, 1999; Heaphy *et al.*, 2003; Weeks, Heaphy and Donovan, 2001; Weston, 1991).

The 'family of choice', as referred to by Weston (1991) and Weeks *et al.* (2001) is, it seems, of crucial importance to older gay men and lesbians in the UK. Heaphy *et al.*'s (2003) study, for example, reported that 53 per cent of women and 49 per cent of men agreed that they perceived friends as family. Finch and Mason (1993) suggested this is a reflection of a number of social developments – the result of which being that family relationships, responsibilities and obligations are in a fluid state of continual negotiation (cited in Weeks *et al.*, 2001: 38). What this perhaps best indicates is that, in the absence of traditional, or at least biological, support systems, older gay men and lesbians have embraced the need to develop and maintain diverse and, arguably, unique networks of support.

The reported lack of biological family support systems on which gay men and lesbians can rely throughout the lifespan may, Berger and Kelly (1986) suggested, actually facilitate successful ageing. Without the taken-for-granted support of biological family members, self-reliance, they argued, is learned at an early age. The role of the gay community has, despite the criticism alluded to above, been reported as being instrumental to the successful ageing of its members. Berger (1982) found that people who were successfully integrated into the gay community were more self-accepting, less depressed and less afraid about the ageing process than those who were more isolated from other gay men and lesbian women.

Similarly, the more recent study undertaken in the UK by Heaphy *et al.* (2003) indicated that lesbian and gay communities were an important source of support for non-heterosexual identities and ways of living. The gay and lesbian community, Heaphy *et al.* (2003: 12) concluded, provided 'a context for the formation of friendships, and social groups and organisations where individuals can "be themselves"'. This conclusion, however, is tempered by the realisation that 'no one is immune to the virus of ageism, and the gay and lesbian community is no exception' (Healey, 1994: 113).

Whilst the early work referred to here appears to have been, at least partially, successful in discrediting many of the myths and stereotypes that abound relating to the lives of older gay men and lesbians, it has, from a methodological perspective, at least, a number of limitations. It tends, for example, to privilege the experience of older gay men (Berger, 1996; Berger and Kelly, 1986; Francher and Henkin, 1973; Friend, 1980; Gray and Dressel, 1985; Kelly, 1977; Kimmel, 1980; Kimmel and Sang, 1995; Kooden, 1997; Sang, Warshow and Smith, 1991), whilst limiting the arguably unique perspective of older lesbians.

In addition, early studies of older gay men and lesbians tend to explore only the 50–69-year age bracket – indeed, as already stated, Berger's (1996) study defined older gay men and those over 40 years of age – and may overlook racial and cultural diversity privileging, in the process, the experience of white, middle-class, affluent individuals living in large urban communities (Cahill *et al.* 2000; Turnbull, 2001: 2). Herdt, Beeler and Rawls (1997: 234) state that 'the combination of poor research literature, clinical samples, and dated historical narratives from prior generations' has had the effect of making the gay and lesbian population seem more homogeneous than it is, thereby 'undercutting diversity in life-course experience'.

This point is echoed more recently by Heaphy (2005: 133) who suggests that future research should not presume that sexual identity is the only one that counts for older gay and lesbian people. He argues for the inclusion of social, cultural and geographical location, ethnicity, the influence of material resources and social supports into future analyses of the lives of gay and lesbian elders.

The homogenising nature of the research referred to here may have other unintended negative effects, one being the inclination to view the lives of older gay men and lesbians as following a linear progression from an identity conceptualised around feelings of shame and guilt from before the gay and lesbian liberation, to an existence that, in the latter half of the twentieth century, was unashamedly 'out and proud'. For some older gay men and lesbians, this is undoubtedly not the case – those who have chosen to continue to conceal their sexual identities or who choose not to identify with terms such as 'lesbian' or 'gay' will continue to lead their very private lives away from the contentious spotlight.

Changes and choices

Whilst some older gay and lesbian people have, undoubtedly, decided to embrace the potential for a less closeted existence presented by changes in the social and political context of gay and lesbian life during the last century, others have, no doubt, decided that a private and contained existence remains the preferred, and safe, option. For them, coming out may never be feasible and, perhaps, the notion of a gay and lesbian community holds little, if any, attraction, having been and most probably remaining a vague and possibly unwelcome constituent of their social milieu. That is, the presumed freedoms generally associated with gay and lesbian liberation may have come as an unwelcome intrusion for those who may have spent many years concealing their true sexual identity for varied reasons and who had fashioned lives based on the concealment of their bona fide sexual selves. These people 'passed' as heterosexual and managed their private and public identities with great skill. For these people the increasing visibility of gay men and lesbians may only have served to exacerbate the possibility and fear of public exposure.

Similarly, recent legislative reforms may, for some, serve only to thrust the issue of sexuality into a more central position in daily life – for those who strive to maintain secrecy and privacy and those who maintain a liberationist rather than assimilationist perspective, these changes may be unwelcome. Indeed, there are those who argue that a purely rights-driven agenda (upon which much recent legislative reform has been predicated), whilst assimilating gay men and lesbians more readily into the day-to-day fabric of civil society, does little to challenge the hegemony of heterosexual privilege or afford gay and lesbian people true equality.

Vaid (1995: 5) suggests, for example, that 'the irony of gay and lesbian mainstreaming is that more than fifty years of active effort to challenge homophobia and heterosexism have yielded us not freedom but "virtual equality"'. Gay and lesbian assimilation, whilst allowing for a perhaps more acceptable social location than complete 'outsider', does not challenge the sexual status quo and, as such, the hegemony of heterosexuality remains unchallenged. Vaid (1995: 5) thus argues that gay and lesbian people are afforded some of the fruits of equality whilst being denied all of its benefits:

> We pay taxes, yet our government denies gay people its public embrace, access to its programs, and its protection…[in short], I believe that the notion that homosexuality has been mainstreamed is an illusion.

She goes on to note that the majority of gay men and lesbians are forced to continue a closeted existence where 'people are still governed primarily by the fear of disclosure of their sexual orientation' (1995: 7). As such, for many people, the social context of gay and lesbian life continues to turn around a fulcrum of heterosexism, defined here as 'an ideological system that denies, denigrates and stigmatizes any non-heterosexual form of behaviour identity, relationship or community' (Herek, 1992: 89). It is in this social and cultural context that gay and lesbian people of all ages continue to lead their lives. For older gay men and lesbians, having lived without the questionable benefits of recent legislative reform, the tyranny of a society that privileges heterosexual sexual identity above any other has been particularly telling.

Heterosexism's most convenient bedfellow, homophobia, remains a clear constituent of the lived experience of many gay men and lesbians and, again, this is a particularly problematic issue when considering the life course of older people. It may mean, for example, that older gay and lesbian people are less likely to access the health and social care services many people routinely require as they age for fear of discrimination, which, in turn, may mean decreased quality of life from both physical and psychological perspectives and an increase in the risk of mortality (Cahill et al., 2000: 17). The effects of heterosexism and homophobia are wide-ranging and potentially affect all areas of a person's life, not least their sense of self, their image and their identity.

Older gay and lesbian people, in a similar vein to their heterosexual counterparts, also worry about the ageing process and its potential connotations. The possibility of needing long-term care, for example, for those who may have felt the necessity to maintain a superficially heteronormative lifestyle, must loom large in terms of anxiety as the onset of disability or long-term illness in later life may be a minefield of potential 'outings'. The crises that may accompany the gradual development of disability, or the diagnosis of life-threatening disease, may mean that previously private matters can suddenly be open to public scrutiny. A person's domestic arrangements and individual living circumstances may be observed and judged in a negative light by those who provide care or treatment and the ability to manage sensitive information about oneself under these circumstances is clearly compromised.

Heaphy *et al.*'s (2003: 12) study found that only 35 per cent of respondents felt health professionals were positive towards non-heterosexual service users and respondents recounted differential treatment, experiences of hostility, and a generalised lack of understanding. They generally understood health and social care providers to operate according to heterosexual assumptions and failed to address their specific needs. In the same report, concern was expressed about residential care provision with 78 per cent of women and 63 per cent of men perceiving residential care as an undesirable option, as there was distrust regarding the extent to which their sexual identities and relationships would be respected in such contexts.

Clearly, whatever the advances in public and political recognition that have occurred for gay men and lesbian women generally, the experience of ageing and its attendant potential for ill health or disability may be the issue that renders ineffectual the carefully constructed coping mechanisms that may have been developed over the years.

Conclusion

It is clear that the cohort of older gay men and lesbians now approaching old age have lived through a tumultuous period of social change. The gay and lesbian liberation movements of the late 1960s and early 1970s and the work of early researchers intent on challenging pejorative stereotypes and images of gay men and lesbians generally, and older gay men and lesbians in particular, brought about radical changes in the way in which gay and lesbian lives were perceived and subsequently constructed – consequently, gay men and lesbians have become a part of the texture of contemporary life. Moreover, the sea change in public and political perceptions that occurred in the 1960s and 1970s undoubtedly presented some gay men and lesbian women with a burgeoning array of potential social identities, whilst also offering opportunities to connect with other like-minded individuals in the nascent gay and lesbian 'community'.

These changes have altered public and political perceptions of homosexuality and have, as a consequence, expanded the range of potential identities available to gay men and lesbians – evidenced by a shift from a limited choice of a identity based on either secrecy or stigma to a choice of social and personal identities that have gradually become part of the mainstream of contemporary society. These changes have been of increasing interest to researchers from the early 1980s, who have charted and influenced public perceptions and political reform.

Reform and social change, however, should not be presumed to affect all gay men and lesbians in similar ways. Some older gay men and lesbian women are willing and able to identify as non-heterosexual in a world that continues to pivot around heterosexual privilege, whilst others choose not to declare their sexual preference. Some older gay and lesbian people have not and will not, therefore, ever 'come out' and those who work with this population of people in old age should be exquisitely sensitive to this.

It is likely that future generations of older gay men and lesbians, used to a degree of public acceptance and political tolerance, will become increasingly vociferous as they age and that, consequently, those who work with this population will be forced to confront, not only heterosexist bias and homophobic practice, but also the necessity to develop truly culturally appropriate and sensitive services. From this perspective, however, it should not be forgotten that there is a group of people who have already aged, who may not identify as gay or lesbian, but who may have long-term and/or committed relationships with others of the same sex. They are the people currently facing the prospect of health and social care provision which, to date, continues to privilege heterosexuality above all other forms of sexual identity. As such, practitioners must be cognisant of the fact that older gay and lesbian people, an already largely invisible population, are easily invalidated and silenced.

Older gay and lesbian people are currently operating at the hub of ageism and heterosexism and, whilst there are arguable advantages related to ageing in a gay or lesbian context, a person's older age, coupled with a non-heterosexual identity, may be the pivot around which oppressive and discriminatory attitudes and practices are allowed to turn in a society which remains reluctant to afford gay and lesbian people, of any age, the simple luxury of true equality.

References

Adelman, M. (1991) 'Stigma, gay lifestyles and adjustment to aging: a study of later life gay men and lesbians.' *Journal of Homosexuality 20*, 3/4, 7–32.

Berger, R.M. (1982) 'The unseen minority: older gays and lesbians.' *Social Work 27*, 3, 236–42.

Berger, R.M. (1996) *Gay and Grey: The Older Homosexual Man.* 2nd edition. New York: Harrington Park Press.

Berger, R.M. and Kelly, J.J. (1986) 'Working with homosexuals of the older population.' *Social Casework 67*, 4, 203–10.

Cahill, S., South, K. and Spade, J. (2000) *Outing Age: Public Policy Issues Affecting Gay, Lesbian, Bisexual and Transgendered Elders.* Washington, DC: The Policy Institute of the National Gay and Lesbian Task Force Foundation.

Carr, S. (2005) '"The Sickness Label Infected Everything We Said": Lesbian and Gay Perspectives on Mental Distress.' In J. Tew (ed.) *Social Perspectives in Mental Health.* London: Jessica Kingsley Publishers.

Deevey, S. (1990) 'Older lesbian women: an invisible minority.' *Journal of Gerontological Nursing 16*, 5, 35–9.

Donovan, C., Heaphy, B. and Weeks, J. (1999) 'Citizenship and same sex relationships.' *Journal of Social Policy 28*, 4, 689–709.

Dorfman, R., Walters, K., Burke, P., Hardin, L., Karanik, T., Raphael, J. and Silverstein, E. (1995) 'Old, sad and alone: the myth of the aging homosexual.' *Journal of Gerontological Social Work 24*, 1/2, 29–44.

Finch, J. and Mason, J. (1993) *Negotiating Family Responsibilities.* London: Routledge.

Foucault, M. (1990) *The History of Sexuality Volume I: An Introduction.* London: Penguin.

Francher, J.S. and Henkin, J. (1973) 'The menopausal queen: adjustment to ageing and the male homosexual.' *American Journal of Orthopsychiatry 43*, 3, 670–4.

Friend, R.A. (1980) 'Gayging: adjustment and the older gay male.' *Alternative Lifestyle 3*, 2, 231–48.

Gray, H. and Dressel, P. (1985) 'Alternative interpretations of aging among gay males.' *The Gerontologist 25*, 1, 83–7.

Healey, S. (1994) 'Diversity with a difference: on being old and lesbian.' *Journal of Gay and Lesbian Social Services 1*, 1, 109–117.

Heaphy, B. (2005) Reviews. *Ageing and Society 25*, 1, 132–4.

Heaphy, B., Yip, A. and Thompson, D. (2003) *Lesbian, Gay and Bisexual Lives Over 50.* Nottingham: York House Publications.

Herdt, G., Beeler, J. and Rawls, T.W. (1997) 'Life course diversity among older lesbians and gay men: a study in Chicago.' *Journal of Gay, Lesbian and Bisexual Identity 2*, 3/4, 231–46.

Herek, G.M. (1992) 'The social context of hate crimes: notes on cultural heterosexism.' In G.M. Herek and K.T. Berrill (eds) *Hate Crimes: Confronting Violence Against Lesbians and Gay Men.* Newbury Park, CA: Sage Publications.

Kehoe, M. (1989) *Lesbians Over 60 Speak for Themselves.* New York: Harrington Park Press.

Kelly, J. (1977) 'The aging male homosexual: myth and reality.' *Gerontologist 17*, 4, 328–32.

Kimmel, D.C. (1978) 'Adult development and aging: a gay perspective.' *Journal of Social Issues 34*, 3, 113–30.

Kimmel, D.C. (1980) 'Life history interview of ageing gay men.' *International Journal of Ageing Human Development 10*, 3, 239–48.

Kimmel, D.C. and Sang, B.E. (1995) 'Lesbians and Gay Men in Midlife.' In A.R. D'Augelli and C.J. Patterson (eds) *Lesbian, Gay and Bisexual Identities Over the Lifespan: Psychological Perspectives.* New York: Oxford University Press.

Kitchen, G. (2003) *Social Care Needs of Older Gay Men and Lesbians on Merseyside.* Liverpool: Ad4design.

Kochman, A. (1997) 'Gay and lesbian elderly: historical overview and implications for social work practice.' *Journal of Gay and Lesbian Social Services 6*, 1, 1–10.

Kooden, H. (1997) 'Successful aging in the middle-aged gay man: a contribution to developmental theory.' *Journal of Gay and Lesbian Social Services 6*, 3, 21–43.

Laner, M.R. (1997) 'Growing older female: heterosexual and homosexual.' *Journal of Lesbian Studies 1*, 1, 87–95.

Langley, J. (2001) 'Developing anti-oppressive empowering social work practice with older lesbian women and gay men.' *British Journal of Social Work 31*, 917–32.

Manthorpe, J. and Price, E. (2006) 'Lesbian carers: personal issues and policy responses.' *Social Policy and Society 5*, 1, 15–26.

Opening Doors in Thanet (2003) *Equally Different: Report on the Situation of Older Lesbian, Gay, Bi-sexual and Transgendered People in Thanet, Kent.* Thanet: Opening Doors in Thanet.

Pugh, S. (2002) 'The Forgotten: A Community without a Generation – Older Lesbians and Gay Men.' In D. Richardson and S. Seidman (eds) *Handbook of Gay and Lesbian Studies.* London: Sage Publications.

Quam, J.K. and Whitford, G.S. (1992) 'Adaptation and Age-Related Expectations of Older Gay and Lesbian Adults.' *The Gerontologist 32*, 3, 357–74.

Rosenfeld, D. (2003) *The Changing of the Guard: Lesbian and Gay Elders, Identity and Social Change.* Philadelphia: Temple University Press.

Sang, B., Warshow, J. and Smith, A.J. *Lesbians at Midlife: The Creative Transition.* Minneapolis, MN: Spinsters Book Company.

Seidman, S. (2004) *Beyond the Closet: The Transformation of Gay and Lesbian Life.* London: Routledge.

Turnbull, A. (2001) *Opening Doors: A Literature Review.* London: Age Concern England.

Vaid, U. (1995) *Virtual Equality: The Mainstreaming of Gay and Lesbian Liberation.* New York: Doubleday.

Weeks, J. (1985) *Sexuality and its Discontents: Meanings, Myths and Modern Sexualities.* London: Routledge.

Weeks, J., Heaphy, B. and Donovan, C. (2001) *Same-Sex Intimacies: Families of Choice and Other Life Experiments.* London: Routledge.

Wellings, K., Field, J., Johnson A.M. and Wadsworth, J. (1994) *Sexual Behaviour in Britain.* London: Penguin.

Weston, K. (1991) *Families We Choose: Lesbians, Gays, Kinship.* New York: Columbia University Press.

Wilton, T. (2000) *Sexualities in Health and Social Care.* Buckingham: Open University Press.

Chapter 7

Constructing Dementia and Dementia Care: Disadvantage and Daily Practices in a Day Care Setting[1]

Jonathan Parker

The idea of everyday practices is important in formulating notions concerning social actions and relations. This is no less the case in dementia care. The concept of practices as used in this chapter is taken from the continuing debate originating in family studies that daily familial practices are constitutive of family. These ideas are applicable more generally to the ways in which everyday practices construct and adapt all social entities. Dementia is considered in terms of its construction by the actions and applied ideas concerning dementia of social care staff practising in a local authority day care setting in the UK. These constructions allow for layers of disadvantage to permeate daily practice at the micro level which reflect structural disadvantages resulting from ageism.

Practices

The beginnings of a concern with everyday practices lie with Bourdieu's (1977) theory of practice. He attempts to explain how the external world is internalised by individuals and how this is reflected back on the world. These structures, which are constitutive of a particular type of environment, produce what Bourdieu terms *habitus*. Habitus are systems of durable, transposable dispositions which orchestrate the generation and structure of practices, or what we do, at an everyday level. Whilst the individual agent is the producer and reproducer of objective meaning, actions and words are often the product of an unconscious assumption and internalisation of external social relations. One of the effects of the habitus is the production, therefore, of a common-sense world endowed with objectivity which is secured by a consensus view of the meaning of certain practices. Bourdieu (1996) applies his ideas to the family. The family as an objective social category is a *structuring structure* – one that helps to create – whilst as a subjective social category it is a *structured structure* – one created by the objective social category. In this sense the objective social category helps to order actions and representations in individual entities which in turn reflect back and reproduce the objective social category.

Practices may result in a group habitus of expectations associated with particular social entities:

> As an acquired system of generative schemes objectively adjusted to the particular conditions in which it is constituted, the habitus engenders all the thoughts, all the perceptions and all the actions consistent with those conditions, and no others. (Bourdieu, 1977: 95)

This articulation of practices can be applied to dementia. The predominant biomedical model of disease and syndrome or even the developing psychosocial approach to dementia may act as an objective social category that structures the meaning of dementia for individuals practising in social and health care settings (Parker, 2003). The received model structures day-to-day care practice and thoughts that explain and justify these actions. These practices – active and cognitive – are then reflected back and reproduce the objective category of dementia found in the biomedical or psychosocial model. Such an understanding of practices may help guard against the reification of a particular conceptualisation and the homogenisation of experiences of dementia, both of which may exclude the individual and his or her own subjective experience. The model may engender practices that, if assumed uncritically, are able to construct assumed disadvantage concerning those with dementia and a lowering of priority or status for those working with people with dementia.

Whilst Bourdieu's theory of practice accounts for the reproduction of social entities and helps us understand how dementia and disadvantage may be constructed between care services and social care workers, it does not seem to account for the possibilities of change and challenge to existing orders (Morgan, 1999). It does not, for instance, account for a shift in paradigm in the last two decades of the twentieth century from the biomedical model to a more psychosocial and person-centred approach to dementia.

It is important not to ignore the academic's involvement in the (re)construction of the concepts and practices studied which militate against or increase the associated disadvantage with working and researching in this area. Smith's (1987) feminist sociological analysis sees practices in a broadly similar way to Bourdieu as ongoing, co-ordering of activities that bring the world into being. She adds the important point, however, that the researcher is also part of the world in which these practices take place, and that knowledge gained or created becomes part of that world. The researcher contributes to the production and reproduction of social entities by her/his involvement and study. The exchange between researcher and researched is constitutive of whatever social entities and processes it is articulated to. Therefore, in the case of dementia care it is necessary to keep in mind that the researcher's or observer's practices and questions are in part constitutive of the subject, that is, dementia. The act of observing, choice of site, biography and predilections of the researcher will influence the data gathered, and the analysis and presentation of them. Thus the researcher may also be an important agent in the construction of entities through the examination of daily practices in a given situation. When this understanding is applied to dementia care practices it is clear that asking the questions produces the potential for action or changed action and can positively impact on raising the status.

Family discourse

Gubrium and Holstein (1990) use the concept of practices in their examination of family as a process rather than an objective or empirical entity. Much of their work is taken from Gubrium's studies in nursing homes and with people with dementia in which professional language is integrated into coherent descriptions of care and external accountability (Gubrium, 1986, 1993). It is therefore directly relevant to the construction of dementia and dementia care. Their research presents meaning to the experiences of care-giving and in terms of how dementia is constructed. They use the term 'family discourse' to describe how meanings are assigned to actions on behalf of social ties. Family discourses are substantive, in respect of ideas, models and theories, and active in communicating how one intends to look at, understand or respond to what is observed (see also Cheal, 1991). In dementia, the substantive and active delineation of practices can also be applied. Substantive practices relate to the received knowledge, ideas, and models that underpin practice and policies. Procedural approaches taken from the developing performance assessment framework (Department of Health, 1999; Department of Health/NHS Executive, 1999), the outworking of legislation for social and health care in the Care Standards Act 2000, NHS Plan (NHS, 2000), and National Service Framework for Older People (Department of Health, 2001) and models and understandings of dementia – either biomedical or person-centred – inform substantive everyday practices in dementia care. Active practices emanate from these in terms of assessment, care plans and delivery in the day-to-day actions of individual practitioners.

Family discourse focuses on 'descriptive practices' (Gubrium and Holstein, 1990: 26). These are situationally sensitive and communicate the processes by which social reality is represented. Family, in this sense, is perceived through its signs using a semiotic approach to metaphor and metonymy (see Adams and Bartlett, 2003). A metaphorical denotation of family makes comparisons with other related conditions, situations or relations. An example of this is given in Gubrium and Holstein's use of Bobbie Glaze's association of bereavement and death with Alzheimer's disease. Family metaphors can also serve as a cultural resource available to monitor the self (see Beck, 1986; Giddens, 1991). This is important in social and health care where moves are increasing to monitor the standards of care (Department of Health, 1999; Department of Health/NHS Executive, 1999; Care Standards Act 2000). Also in the development of best practice in dementia care and person-centred approaches (Benson, 2000; Kitwood, 1997), the models received and assimilated can be used to monitor practice and the use of self in dementia care. The 'yardstick' perhaps changes from how long is spent on completing physical tasks to how long one engages socially with a person with dementia (Parker, 2001).

Gubrium and Holstein (1990) also identify a metonymical denotation of family in which a commonly associated feature of family is used to designate family itself. Again, in dementia care denotation of dementia is seen in substantive and active ways. In the attitudes and views expressed, and considerations of ability and capacity, people with dementia are conceptualised as being childlike in abilities and needs and practices accordingly can be seen to limit and infantilise when such views are acted upon. Indeed, many people with dementia are defined by risks resulting from incapacity and loss of memory.

Family and everyday practices

It is with Morgan (1996, 1999) that the clearest articulation of practices is given, although, again, he uses the term in respect of family. He challenges the uncritical usage of the term 'family' as potentially rigidifying and normalising and we may perhaps recognise the same problems in respect of terms such as 'care' and 'carer' in respect of people with dementia. Popular and policy-oriented accounts of the family often lack the fluidity and diversity observed in society. These accounts produce lists of various elements in which the reader is invited to link entities and identify these entities with the assembly of material collected. The suggestion is made that characteristics of social entities are open to tabulation and quantification. Morgan (1996, 1999) suggests rather that 'family' should be understood as an adjective or even a verb.

Practices draw upon common-sense, everyday understandings and how these are used reflexively to structure that world. Bernades (1997) adds that they also demarcate from practices not assumed or considered to be part of that site of practice. In terms of dementia and dementia care, it is evident that these understandings have relevance. Dementia is assumed to represent an organic disease entity made manifest by certain behaviours. This becomes the norm against which other practices and articulations fall short. It may be in social and health care that psychosocial approaches based on personhood also build an architecture of dementia and dementia care against which other approaches are disregarded or made deviant.

Dementia can be understood in an active sense. Meaning is given in the practices associated with care given. To some extent this has been under-taken previously by accounts which conceptualise dementia according to behaviours observed. Wandering, anxiety, restlessness and aggression have all been linked to dementia. Daily practices constitutive of dementia care include the responses made to these behaviours in the context in which they occur. This context is itself influenced by normative ideas of the concept of dementia, for instance as a particular disease entity or as an observable set of behaviours displayed under certain conditions. Those working with dementia are in this sense working with 'deviance' and as champions are themselves associated with that deviance. Care-giving goes further still and the assumption of such constructions leads to a hierarchical division of worth and a degree of resistance between the levels of care staff.

The lower status accorded to care work (Jack, 1994), partly as a result of the negative images associated with bodywork (Twigg, 2000), reflects an understanding in respect of dementia as being outside the viable, the normal and the wished-for. Daily practices focusing on the body in dementia care may perhaps add to the negative construction of dementia and dementia care.

Morgan (1996) developed further the idea of family practices and sug-gested that they were not bounded by the usually expected confines of the family. In fact, '(t)heir significance derives from their location in wider systems of meaning' (Morgan, 1996: 190). Family practices, as opposed to *the* family, represent processes that interact with other areas of social enquiry. This avoids the potentially dangerous reification of family in terms of policy constructing normative standards against which others are seen as deviant. This is important to note. Practices constitutive of dementia and dementia care are not bounded by the institutions in which direct care is provided. The gendered nature of the workforce (Arber and Ginn, 1991; Jack, 1994), the training and qualifications provided (TOPSS, 2000), the location and status of social care in relation to health care, and the personal biographies of individual care staff are important in (re)producing systems of dementia care. Understanding this, we can begin to challenge the disadvantages experienced by social care staff that reflect the ageism and able-ism experienced by people with dementia.

In general, practices are defined by the social actors involved, but this is not considered the sole criterion of definition. These definitions might not always be available to the observer. For instance, it might not be possible for one person with dementia to communicate their meaning of dementia to another. Practices are concerned with cognitive constructions but also with the significance for those parties involved. They are 'a way of looking at, and describing, practices which might also be described in a variety of other ways' (Morgan, 1996: 199). Practices can, therefore, be described by others involved in an observational or descriptive role.

Morgan (1999) sees that there are three sets of agencies involved in constructing family practices. First, as we have mentioned above, the social actors involved in the social entity themselves make links between activities and general notions of family. These linkages, activities and notions are constantly negotiated and redefined by individual experience and reflection. Second, more abstract agencies are involved. These may include professionals, moral and religious agencies, policy-makers and the like. Distinctions are made in these pronouncements between family and non-family, between positive and negative, included and excluded. These professional accounts are influential to individuals and may build a cultural resource which provides meaning for the individual care practitioner, or, indeed, the recipients of that care and their families. There is a reflexive monitoring of one's own routine practices against some standard of normality which becomes reproductive of those standards. The final agency involved in the construction of practices is the observer, as stressed by Smith (1987). Morgan suggests that observers are often ignored in discussions of social construction. It is routinely experienced that the constructions of observers should match and derive from those of the actors whose practices are being described. This is not always the case and observer effects/notions/constructions are important.

The term *practices* conveys a range of related themes:

1. A sense of interplay between the perspectives of the social actor, the individual whose actions are being described and accounted for and the perspectives of the observer (Morgan, 1999: 17). The concept of practices emphasises that there are different perspectives and interpretations.

2. A sense of active rather than passive or static (Morgan, 1999: 17). There is a sense of 'doing' which both constitutes and derives from notions of family and proper conduct between family members.

3. A focus on the everyday (Morgan, 1999: 17). There is a concern with the routine and trivial as part of how family life is seen.

4. A stress on regularities (Morgan, 1999: 17). Regularities or repeated actions that constitute part of the everyday taken-for-granted worlds.

5. A sense of fluidity (Morgan, 1999: 18). Practices are not bounded but flow into other practices that are similar or different.

6. An interplay between history and biography (Morgan, 1999: 18). Practices have societal and historical dimensions as well as concern with the everyday and here-and-now.

Harding and Palfrey (1997) describe how dementia has been socially constructed as a disease entity. This model has dominated the minds of service providers, planners and health and social care (Cheston and Bender, 1999). The work of Kitwood concerning the dialectical interplay of neurological impairment and what he termed 'malignant social psychology' provides a useful model to understand the processes in which dementia becomes known and worked with by the ascriptions associated with it (Davis, 2004; Kitwood, 1990; Kitwood, 1993; Kitwood, 1997). The social constructionist debate has also evolved in respect of the importance of the person and his or her voice in dementia care (Adams, 2001a, 2001b; Bender and Cheston, 1997; Downs, 1997; Sabat and Harré, 1992). Cheston and Bender (1999) progress the model and demonstrate its application to social and health care practice. It is in the context of everyday practices, however, that an understanding of the social construction of dementia is important.

Practices represent a way of conceptualising the fluidity of social life as a point of departure. Practices allow for a variety of different perspectives and to consider subjects through a variety of different lenses. External practices may reinforce or construct notions of the social entity described. They are associated with wider understandings of the world and, as we have seen, do not necessarily take place in times and spaces that are conventionally designated to do with the entity described. Thus the site of dementia care may not be the only place in which dementia is constructed. In the biographies of workers, and their family experiences, dementia takes on meaning. The role of social care practitioner in his or her family and the family's experience of dementia are important considerations relating to the continued construction of dementia and dementia care in everyday practices.

The study

The data for this study are taken from observations of the daily practices of, and interviews with, social care staff working with people with dementia in a local authority day centre in the UK. The study is limited, therefore, in scope and range. A larger study would need to consider practices external to those designated for the purpose of care and examine the language used concerning dementia. However, the everyday social care practices in this day centre provide data that begin to reflect the ways in which dementia and dementia care are constructed in this particular setting. The study is therefore descriptive rather than representative. The data are analysed by reference to the concept of practices across a range of constructive levels and domains deriving from the data. A process of axial and selective coding was used to make connections between observed practices, perceptions of care and dementia care (see Strauss and Corbin, 1990).

It is the case that representations of practices are organisationally embedded. They are situationally specific and their articulation is embedded in local discursive conventions. Agents are 'constantly interpreting the recognisable features of everyday life, sifting through cultural instructions, articulating available models with everyday experiences to assemble the coherent social realities they inhabit' (Gubrium and Holstein, 1990: 117; Gubrium and Holstein, 1993). The object of descriptive practice is interpreted and assembled out of experience. Those involved in the site of practice are often assumed to have the most authentic knowledge of the site. This claim to privileged knowledge is used in two ways to warrant the claims of members and to discount outside opinion. Questions of ontology, what the practices are, and epistemology, how we know these practices, are also raised. In day care, this is certainly given evidence in comments about senior care officers and management, change, other groups of staff and sites of practice.

The findings

The physical environment and setting

The purpose-built day care centre, in which the study was conducted, has one large room with a separate staff room at one end by which care staff enter and leave but they cannot be seen inside it nor can they overlook activities that are ongoing. There is a serving hatch at one side from which food is served. The main office is situated at the end of the room. The room, people and activities can be observed from this space (see Figure 7.1 for the layout).

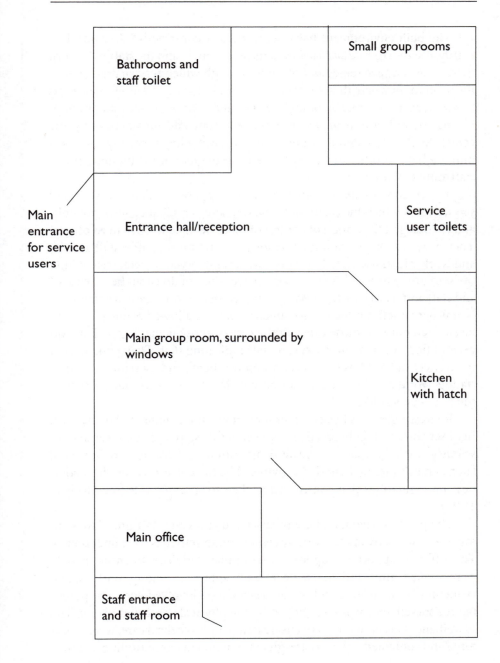

Figure 7.1 Plan of day centre

The entrance hall is fairly large. Rooms off the entrance hall include lavatories for day care service users en route to the main room. The other corridor contains a small group/meeting room, a kitchen for service users, bathing and physiotherapy areas, and staff lavatories.

The built environment has three particular constructive domains. Primarily, it serves to *hold and homogenise* its service users and the staff who work there. The entrance serves as a conduit, through which service users pass to the main room where they sit, eat and undertake group activities. It also acts to *demarcate and distance* by bounding staff and member space and developing the shared notion of distance between staff and members using the centre. Staff only entered through this entrance when escorting members into the hall. At other times, staff entered at the rear of the building into a staff-only environment.

The bounded nature of space created a separation between staff and service users which meant that observation and surveillance were possible, and encouraged the notion of control of those deemed to be in need of care. There way also the possibility of senior staff monitoring junior staff activity and work which was noted by care workers and served to demarcate within the staff group itself. This fed into the perceptions of divisions between staff and staff and staff and service user, allowing staff members to offer care in a standardised way that left out the service users' views and allowed blame for this to be situated outwith those offering the care or those managing it. This was exemplified in comments from care staff indicating that 'They [attendees at the day centre] need us to do everything for them', and by senior care staff stating 'We try to be person-centred but they [junior care staff] just treat them [attendees] like children.'

Interestingly, the physical environment was not commented on by staff. In observations of daily practice it appeared that staff and attendees unconsciously used the space to create demarcation by herding activities and, later, at mealtimes by bounded activities. The focus was on everyday activities and regularities that constituted a taken-for-granted role (see Morgan, 1996).

The physical layout and use of space did allow the staff group to work together, especially in the mornings when group activities were undertaken. This offered support and opportunities to plan activities, to ensure people were looked after and to create a team approach among staff. Again, elements of demarcation and *care and control* were involved here. The potential for surveillance was emphasised by the physical space and its use. The surveillance was undertaken to ensure that people received care, were monitored and contained. It had a care-giving function in its controlling action.

Routines and activities
Staff time was used in a planned way to deliver systematic programmes of day care. This led to a degree of regimentation on arrival for people attending

the day centre. They were all greeted by being given a name badge and having a cup of tea; this was followed by group activities for all service users together, lunch, and smaller group activities in the afternoon. The implicit assumption seemed to be that this constituted appropriate activities for the service user group, who required regularity: an activity-focused day led by staff and undertaken by service users. These actions were constitutive of an overall construction of dementia and dementia care.

However, there were discrepancies in how staff undertook these functions depending, to some extent, on the position, training and life experiences of care staff. Senior care staff generally expected a greater level of involvement and capacity from service users and had higher levels of training. Personal or familial experiences of dementia had an impact on junior and senior care staff. Approaches to service users ranged from cajoling all to join in, to providing individual activities, where possible, for those who did not wish to join in. At times group activities were dominated by the more confident and competent service users which detracted from the experiences of those who were unable to participate as actively. This tended to demarcate those with a greater degree of cognitive ability from those with less:

> A daily diary is completed whilst most members sit around the white board... However, I feel the daily diary slot is dominated by the more vocal service users with the least signs of dementia...

Some staff actively encouraged this, suggesting that it allowed those who could join in to get more from the activities and thus prevented them from becoming frustrated. There was a degree of disagreement between those constructing the plans for activities and those delivering them which seemed to be bound up with the routinised expectations of deliverers rather than the fluid potential of planners.

Also, the systematic, planned approach at times excluded members. One woman was left out of smaller group activities because her name had been left off the list. She remained unoccupied and mainly unattended until this was noticed. The following quotation from a care officer demonstrates the discrepancies in planning and delivery:

> One lady, Flora [not her real name], was left out from the groups, as her name was not written down and assigned to a group activity. I sat and talked with Flora for about five minutes before [another member of staff] came and said she could join their group.

Activities and work within the centre with service users was constrained by the working hours of staff (generally 8.30 a.m. to 4 p.m.), the timing of the transport bringing service users, and refreshments and meals. The greatest constraint was the transport which collected and returned two groups of people from a wide area of a city often travelling for over one hour without there being guaranteed times for arrival or departure. This curtailed activities and often led to disquiet. Special needs were not accounted for in this and transport served to herd and homogenise the groups of service users by geography. Needs were assumed to be the same for each member and their families. However, care staff were aware of the problems raised by issues of transport considering them in the light of their own life settings and perceived expectations, as the following statements from practitioners show:

> ...transport is abysmal. Those picked up last are generally taken home first. Those picked up first have longer to spend on the bus. I would expect a full day's break...

> The transport bus usually takes two runs each day but there is no continuity with the escort – one bus went to pick up someone who had died!

> ...activities didn't begin until 11.40 so people arriving on the first bus just sat waiting for the second bus to arrive...she seemed to be saying she had wasted the morning and resented those coming on the second bus for causing this...

Issues of and difficulties with transport have been noted as a matter of concern by the Social Services Inspectorate report *At Home with Dementia* (SSI/DoH, 1997: 3, 5):

> Transport arrangements sometimes undermined the potential value of some services for older people with dementia, most usually because of their failure to respond to the needs of individual users and carers.

> SSDs [social services departments] should monitor and review transport arrangements to ensure that they meet the needs of service users as efficiently and effectively as possible.

Meals tended to define the day in a number of ways. Staff tended to serve the meals, lay tables and clear away 'because it's easier like that', and service users seemed to be the passive recipients. This suited many who appreciated the 'hotel' aspect of the experience, but others who wished to help were not actively encouraged to do so. People were treated according to their status as service users rather than their desire to join in, to be consulted or, indeed, according to their abilities. This belied another distinction creating distance between staff and service users and reflected a homogenising construction that service users were in need of care and control by staff. Staff had lunch in two sittings after service users. Again, this emphasised the cared-for positioning of service users and separated staff from them.

Daily routines and activities were given emphasis at senior care-worker level and planning, designing and implementing activity and group work were considered to be high priorities. However, this created some disillusionment amongst care staff as demonstrated in the following quotation:

> There is no real vision of where [the centre] is going except to provide relief. Daily routine is left to care workers and the different views of seniors. The four-week plans were useful in designing topics...not work because care officers wanted to choose their own topics and not everyone has the same skills.

Planning for activities was undertaken in a hierarchical manner by senior care staff who planned weekly activity schedules which were then passed on to care officers to implement. The activities took into account the training needs of care staff, including opportunities for NVQ assessment.[2] Activities were, therefore, consistent with staff development plans and, by default, with contemporary theories concerning positive dementia care and person-centred approaches. Activities included creative methods of communication using words, pictures and objects; reminiscence work; and poetry workshops, as well as the more traditional reality orientation quizzes.

In everyday practice, these plans were hampered by staff sickness, leave, perceived low numbers of staff and the contention that senior staff should be responsible for such planning because they were paid more. Senior care staff did not all have the same views. Within the staff teams there was a tension also, as shown by the following statement made by a care officer:

> Clients are entertained by attending. When they are not this is because of a lack of time and planning for individuals. There is a great need for more staff and clearer boundaries between workers and officers; a lot is expected of care officers and abilities are mixed.

Group activities were set for all service users in the morning and consisted of simple cognitive exercises concerning diary events, names and quizzes, and some gentle physical activity. There was no account taken of those who did not want to join in and, at times, there was a gendered approach to activities which was felt to exclude male service users. This is something recognised as an issue across social care:

> SSDs need to consider the extent to which their equal opportunity policies address the gender needs of service users. They should also ensure that service providers have an appropriate mix of staff to deliver gender appropriate care in practice. (SSI/DoH, 1997: 6)

Afternoon activities were planned with specific interests and needs in mind. Smaller groups were organised and some degree of participation in planning was possible, although this was mainly led by staff interests. Staff brought a range of perspectives from day care, residential care, NVQ training, wider experiences and family life. These influenced the construction and delivery of day care. Care-giving gave a sense of satisfaction for staff and there was an explicitly stated desire to offer activities determined by service users and to ensure that these were age appropriate. This did not always happen with service users sometimes receiving the same input regardless. The question of training and competence seemed to demarcate staff:

> Groups are designed for the client and matching takes place. But often staff want to be told what to do and not have to think and decide... The care is there but the stimulation needs more support – groups and plans. There is a need for formal training but also for reflecting on experience and recognising what others do well.

The training and position of staff impacted on practices and beliefs underlying them. Senior care officers were generally undertaking training at a formal level (NVQ) but were reading around the literature to inform practice and had assimilated concepts of well-being and positive communication practice. The managerial responsibilities of staff tended to take senior care staff away from much direct contact with attendees which was then passed down to junior care staff. These care officers were less likely to be involved in formal training post-induction or, at times, Level 2 NVQ. The views of dementia they brought to the work derived from personal experience in a more explicit way and from embedded constructs from traditional approaches to care work. Amongst those with direct contact responsibility there appeared to be an unquestioning acceptance of the inevitable deterioration and need for active imposed care of people with dementia. One member of staff argued:

> Well, it's all right for them [senior care staff] to have these ideas, but they [attendees] need our help; they're just like children whatever you say.

This view seemed to permeate interactions that were of the order of 'doing to' rather than 'doing with'. For example, this was not only the case at mealtimes, but also, when toileting, members were approached in a way that was sensitive but demonstrative. People were helped physically and walked to the toilet as a matter of course, although senior staff were adamant that individual need should determine these actions.

Discussion

Understanding and training remained at a superficial level reflecting histor-ical approaches to social care staff, and the privileging of core social care areas to the disadvantage of others. Whilst training had been undertaken amongst senior care and care staff concerning the development of positive approaches to dementia care and person-centred ways of working (Kitwood and Benson, 1995; Parker and Penhale, 1998; Stokes, 1987, a b, c, d), old habits remained. The person with dementia was seen as impaired, in need, deteriorating – in terms of their weaknesses and illness – rather than as a person. This has great implications for training and development. Indeed, it seems as though there was, at times, a bi-directional assertion of deviance, with senior care staff assuming greater knowledge and suggesting that care officers should give up their old assumptions, whilst care staff in more junior positions castigated the views of senior staff by stating that their views were idealistic and not grounded in daily realities (see Bernades, 1997). If there were any observer effect on the practices of care staff this indicates further the need for training.

In order to understand some of the ways in which dementia and dementia care was constructed in this setting a number of levels of practice and construction were identified from the observations made and inter-views undertaken. These concerned the physical environment, a cognitive and intellectual level and an emotional/personal level. At each level of practice and construction, a number of constructive domains were noted. These overlapped across levels and included 'holding and homogenising', 'demarcating and distancing' and 'care-giving and control'. These domains of practice illustrated how dementia was understood, as a disease affecting others who will need care and control, and how dementia care was done. This was similar to Morgan's (1996) view of family as an adjective or verb as opposed to static noun. The context in which these practices and construc-tions were made was also important. Dementia was seen to be constructed on these three interacting levels which were in turn influenced by the context of social care history, change and the individual experiences of the care staff. The experiences of care staff are not bounded solely by history. Their individual knowledge, experience, training and interpretation are important in the co-construction of day care and dementia within that context. This model of construction is shown in Figure 7.2. It is also possible that the historical context of social care provides a rationale for purpose-built centres that reflect the 'holding' and 'distancing' functions and do not fit comfortably with contemporary constructions of care but still inform many of the everyday practices observed.

Constructive levels

Historical context   Biographical context

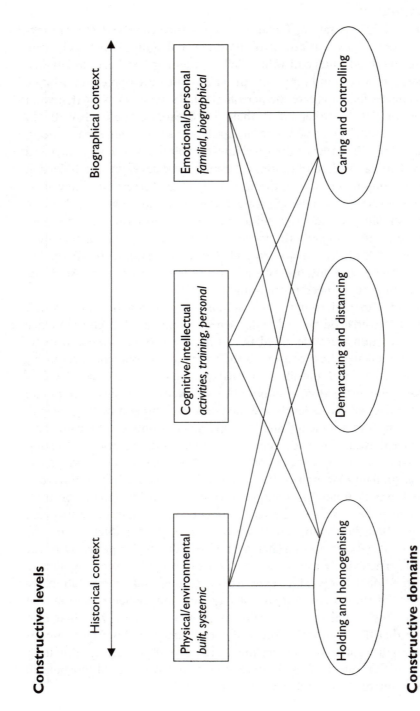

Constructive domains

Figure 7.2 Constructing dementia in the day care setting

Daily practices recreate dementia and dementia care because of their regularised nature and specific function as a centre for dementia care. The activities and attitudes promoted are associated with the condition. This is clear in respect of the care-giving, regulated aspects of the centre and in the planning and implementation of activities. However, these constructions are not fixed but are open to change and development by interaction, interpreting difference and challenge. The overall importance of daily practices lies in the potential for planning services, training staff and ensuring that an ethic of social care is promoted. The generalising and homogenising principles of social care evident in this particular study are potentially exclusive of individuals and their worth. Making transparent the practices and meanings derived from them helps to identify training needs and aspects of practice for change, and highlights the importance of ethical approaches to practice.

It is important to remember that the construction and reconstruction of practices is multidirectional and influence at each level can produce effects at other levels (Bourdieu, 1996). Policies, procedures and working methods influence practice but, also, the expectations and daily routines of each practice site reflect back on to policy-makers. It is especially important to attend to the personal biographies of staff to provide a supportive environment that encourages reflection on practice and the development of approaches that take cognisance of the individual needs of the person with dementia (Kitwood, 1997). In this study, biographies appeared to be used in two ways. First, there was a historical use in which care staff used personal and familial experiences to affect their views of how care should be delivered: a projection of what one would want for one's own relatives or oneself, which often related to caring and controlling approaches to practice. Second, there was a more contemporaneous use of personal development and training. Unfortunately, at times this development seemed to be concerned with a 'professionalising' tendency that demarcated and distanced staff from service users, and a position that demarcated staff groups and reconstructed assumptions of disadvantage and lack of worth. What seemed to be lacking was a reflexive and future-oriented developmental approach. This, again, suggests that training is needed, not only in understanding the concepts of person-centred care but also in the implementation of a new culture. However, to suggest that this was the result of individual care staff experiences alone would exclude the significance of structural and organisational aspects of care delivery. The given nature of day care did not seem to be questioned and this had an impact on the approaches to individual practice. Traditional models of dementia seemed to become embedded when a personal experience of dementia confirmed to the individual that a caring and controlling approach to service users was necessary. This tended to homogenise individuals' constructions of dementia and impact upon their practice.

The ways in which we approach, engage with and talk about people convey a sense of how we interpret their situations. This informs our practices and the practices of others and becomes embedded as part of the assumptive world when dealing with people. As moves are made more widely to improve and enhance dementia care, it is important that practices demonstrate the new culture of care, not only the words spoken about it. We may be able to achieve this cultural shift more readily if we accept that we construct our practices in our interactions with others and that those practices can be fluid and lead to development and change. If we take our starting point as respect for individual staff members in social care and their biography alongside respect for service users and their carers, this new culture may become more of a reality.

Notes

1   A version of this chapter was published in the *Journal of Social Work Practice 5*, 3, for which the copyright is held by Sage Publications.

2   National Vocational Qualifications (NVQs) form an important continuum of formally recognised training designed to up-skill the social care workforce.

References

Adams, T. (2001a) 'The social construction of risk by community psychiatric nurses and family carers for people with dementia.' *Health, Risk and Society 3*, 3, 307–19.

Adams, T. (2001b) 'The conversational and discursive construction of psychiatric nursing for chronically confused people and their families.' *Nursing Inquiry 8*, 2, 98–107.

Adams, T. and Bartlett, R. (2003) 'Constructing Dementia.' In T. Adams and J. Manthorpe (eds) *Dementia Care*. London: Arnold.

Arber, S. and Ginn, J. (1991) *Gender and Later Life*. London: Sage.

Beck, U. (1986) *Risikogesellschaft: Auf dem Weg in eine andere Moderne*. Frankfurt: Suhrkamp.

Bender, M. and Cheston, R. (1997) 'Inhabitants of a lost kingdom: a model of the subjective experiences of dementia.' *Ageing and Society 17*, 513–32.

Benson, S. (ed.) (2000) *Person-Centred Care: Creative Approaches to Individualised Care for People with Dementia*. London: Hawker Publications.

Bernades, J. (1997) *Family Studies: An Introduction*. London: Routledge.

Bourdieu, P. (1977) *Outline of a Theory of Practice*. Cambridge: Cambridge University Press.

Bourdieu, P. (1996) 'On the family as a realized category.' *Theory, Culture and Society 13*, 19–26.

Cheal, D. (1991) *Family and the State of Theory*. Toronto: University of Toronto Press.

Cheston, R. and Bender, M. (1999) *Understanding Dementia: The Man with the Worried Eyes*. London: Jessica Kingsley Publishers.

Davis, D. (2004) 'Dementia: sociological and philosophical constructions.' *Social Science and Medicine 58*, 2, 369–78.

Department of Health (1999) *A New Approach to Social Services Performance*. London: Department of Health.

Department of Health (2001) *National Service Framework for Older People*. London: Stationery Office.

Department of Health/NHS Executive (1999) *The NHS Performance Assessment Framework.* London: Department of Health.

Downs, M. (1997) 'The emergence of the person on dementia research.' *Ageing and Society 17,* 597–607.

Giddens, A. (1991) *Modernity and Self-Identity: Self and Society in the Late Modern Age.* Cambridge: Polity Press.

Gubrium, J.F. (1986) *Oldtimers and Alzheimer's: The Descriptive Organization of Senility.* London: JAI Press.

Gubrium, J.F. (1993) *Speaking of a Life: Horizons of Meaning for Nursing Home Residents.* New York: Adline de Gruyter.

Gubrium, J. and Holstein, J. (1990) *What is Family?* Mountain View, CA: Mayfield Publishing Co.

Gubrium, J. and Holstein, J. (1993) 'Family discourse, organizational embeddedness, and local enactment.' *Journal of Family Issues 14,* 66–82.

Harding, N. and Palfrey, C. (1997) *The Social Construction of Dementia.* London: Jessica Kingsley Publishers.

Jack, R. (1994) 'Dependence, Power And Violation: Gender Issues in Abuse of Elderly People by Informal Carers.' In M. Eastman (ed.) *Old Age Abuse: A New Perspective.* 2nd edition. London: Chapman Hall.

Kitwood, T. (1990) 'The dialectics of dementia: with particular reference to Alzheimer's disease.' *Ageing and Society 10,* 177–96.

Kitwood, T. (1993) 'Towards a theory of dementia care: the interpersonal process.' *Ageing and Society 13,* 51–67.

Kitwood, T. (1997) *Dementia Reconsidered: The Person Comes First.* Buckingham: Open University Press.

Kitwood, T. and Benson, S. (eds) (1995) *The New Culture of Dementia Care.* London: Hawker Publications.

Morgan, D. (1996) *Family Connections.* Cambridge: Polity Press.

Morgan, D. (1999) 'Risk and Family Practices: Accounting for Change and Fluidity in Family Life.' In E.B. Silva and C. Smart (eds) *The New Family.* London: Sage.

NHS (2000) *The NHS Plan: A Plan for Investment. A Plan for Reform.* Cm 4818-1. London: HMSO.

Parker, J. (2001) 'Interrogating person-centred dementia care in social work and social care.' *Journal of Social Work 1,* 3, 329–45.

Parker, J. (2003) 'Positive Communication with People who have Dementia.' In T. Adams and J. Manthorpe (eds) *Dementia Care.* London: Arnold.

Parker, J. and Penhale, B. (1998) *Forgotten People: Positive Approaches to Dementia Care.* Aldershot: Arena.

Sabat, S.R. and Harré, R. (1992) 'The construction and deconstruction of self in Alzheimer's disease.' *Ageing and Society 12,* 443–61.

Smith, D.E. (1987) *The Everyday World as Problematic: A Feminist Sociology.* Boston, MA: Northeastern University Press.

SSI/DoH (1997) *At Home with Dementia: Inspection of Services for Older People with Dementia in the Community, 1996.* London: HMSO.

Stokes, G. (1987a) *Aggression.* Bicester: Winslow Press.

Stokes, G. (1987b) *Incontinence and Inappropriate Urinating.* Bicester: Winslow Press.

Stokes, G. (1987c) *Screaming and Shouting.* Bicester: Winslow Press.

Stokes, G. (1987d) *Wandering.* Bicester: Winslow Press.

Strauss, A. and Corbin, J. (1990) *Basics of Qualitative Research: Grounded Theory Procedure and Techniques.* Newbury Park: Sage.

TOPSS (2000) *Modernising the Social Care Workforce – The First National Training Strategy for England.* Leeds: TOPSS England.

Twigg, J. (2000) 'Carework as a form of bodywork.' *Ageing and Society 20,* 389–411.

Chapter 8

Living with Chronic Illness: The Example of Parkinson's Disease

Margaret Holloway[1]

Living with chronic illness is an all-pervasive experience for the individual who has the illness and for their family members. Sickness and health, disability and capability, giving and receiving care, are intricately and intimately bound together in the minutiae of everyday life – for both the one who has the illness and for their partners, carers and other family members. The sociology of health and illness literature has long recognised that illness is more than physical sickness (Scambler and Higgs, 1998). We are familiar with notions such as the 'burden of illness', which characterises illness as an ongoing and cumulative struggle (e.g. Anderson and Bury, 1988). The psychological impact and consequent reconstruction of the self through the taking on of a new identity and altered biography are encapsulated in the concepts of 'biographical disruption' (Bury, 1997) and 'illness narrative' (Radley, 1993). Parson's work on social role theory has been enthusiastically applied to the way in which individuals fulfil the 'sick role' in any social grouping, especially the family (e.g. Walmsley *et al.*, 1992). The emotional consequences of the losses associated with disability and illness have been explored, sometimes, as the social model of disability has pointed out, in complete distortion of the way in which the individuals themselves see their lives (Oliver and Sapey, 1999). The association between disability and poverty has been repeatedly highlighted by social policy commentators (e.g. Oliver and Barnes, 1998; Walker and Townsend, 1981). Yet the experiences of aggregated disadvantage and stigmatisation, which for many people living with chronic illness are amongst its most marked effects and constant reminders of its presence, have been relatively ignored in the literature (see Locker, 1983, for an early exception to this).

The example of Parkinson's disease on which this chapter focuses provides us with ample illustration of the disadvantage and stigma experienced not only by the person who has Parkinson's but also their immediate family and carers. Parkinson's disease affects around 120,000 people in the UK (1 in 500 of the population) and an estimated four million people worldwide (www.parkinsons.org.uk). Of particular significance is the fact that the incidence of the disease rises with age and we are thus looking at a significant group of people made frail and vulnerable by a combination of age, disability and serious health problems. One European study reported prevalence rates of 2.3 per cent for Parkinsonism and 1.6 per cent for Parkinson's disease itself in populations over 65 years. Given that the most powerful determinant of the disease is old age itself, these figures are set to rise as populations age (Meara and Hobson, 2000). In the UK, 70 per cent of those with Parkinson's are estimated to be over the age of 70. The majority of these are living with a similarly aged spouse (Yarrow, 1999) many of whom have age-related health problems (Lloyd, 1999). Growing numbers of people surviving into old age, coupled with a disease whose incidence rises sharply with age, mean that the effects of such an illness for some of the most frail older people are increasingly a factor with which a range of health and social care service providers must reckon.

Parkinson's is a chronic, progressive disease for which there is no known cure. Its progress is unpredictable in the longer term and at the same time it is experienced in the present as a highly variable, fluctuating condition. This factor alone is enough to create attendant emotional problems and, as with any illness, its effects are never purely physical and rarely confined to the person who has the illness. Yet there can be times and stages when the physical symptoms are mild and so successfully controlled by medication that the effect on the person's life as a whole is minimal. At other times, it can seem that everything the person does, thinks and feels is dominated by the effects of a highly disabling illness. These effects are inevitably experienced by those who share the life of the person with Parkinson's. In Parkinson's disease, as with many illnesses, it is the physical symptoms which receive the most attention from professionals, but it is the social and emotional impact of those physical problems which may have the greatest effect on the carer or family member. Exploring the relationship between physical problems and needs, and social and emotional problems and needs, for people with Parkinson's and their families, demonstrates how the experience of illness is socially constructed and that the burden of that illness is as much imposed by society as it is a consequence of physical limitation.

This chapter will explore the impact of associated stigma and disadvantage for the families of people with Parkinson's disease. However, the experience it conveys is one which will be familiar to a wide range of people and their families living with chronic, disabling illness. The chapter draws on two research studies conducted by the author. The first was a mixed methods study of community care for people with Parkinson's disease and their carers, which utilised a postal questionnaire survey (202 respondents with Parkinson's, 140 carers). The second, a pilot study of a user-led care pathway developed out of the recommendations from the community care study, followed the progress of 22 people with Parkinson's, most of whom had a live-in carer, over a 12-month period during which they used the care pathway tools developed; this study collected mostly qualitative data. The methods and findings of these studies have been fully reported in both study reports (Lloyd, 2002; Lloyd and Smith, 1998) and in previously published work (Lloyd, 1999 and 2000; Holloway, 2006). This chapter uses selected data from both studies to illustrate and highlight the arguments concerning associated disadvantage and stigma.

Although most people think of Parkinson's disease as 'the shaking disease' (if they have any knowledge of it at all), there are in fact a number of physical symptoms commonly experienced. These include fatigue, walking, bowel and bladder problems, speech difficulties, dribbling and difficulty swallowing, as well as the commonly recognised tremor. These are all problems that have social implications for the person with Parkinson's and her or his family. Respondents in the community care survey were asked to rate the degree of difficulty they experienced in these areas. Their answers revealed that significant numbers experienced at least some difficulty with all these symptoms with tiredness, walking and tremor emerging as the main problem areas. Sixty-one per cent said that tiredness was a major problem for them and 56 per cent experienced a lot of difficulty with walking. Both the people with Parkinson's themselves, and their family members, emphasised the social impact of these physical problems in terms of the disadvantage and restrictions imposed on them. The practical effects of such physical problems in terms of daily living are significant, but so too are the knock-on social and emotional consequences, not only for the person who has the symptoms but also for their carers.

Mobility problems
Ninety-three per cent of the people with Parkinson's in this community care study had problems with mobility inside and outside of the home. This man described the effects of this as much in terms of its social and emotional impact as the practical consequences:

The long periods of immobility are soul-destroying... I can sense myself changing when I become immobile, also the way friends and relatives react to me.

This woman and her daughter carer express two sides of the same coin:

From being a very active person to now, I can hardly walk. Terrible when it comes on you. (Woman with Parkinson's)

She's deteriorated so much in the last two years and I mean that whole-heartedly... In another 12 months this house is going to be a prison for her. (Daughter)

Carers too reflected the social and emotional consequences arising out of the mobility problems experienced by the person with Parkinson's. Sixty-seven per cent of carers stated that they gave some degree of help to the person with Parkinson's in getting around the house, and 75 per cent said that they needed to help with mobility outside the home. This affected the freedom and independence of both parties:

She wants to come everywhere with me because I am her lifeline. She wouldn't get out otherwise. (Carer)

One unexpected but striking attendant social consequence for those people with Parkinson's who had significant mobility problems was that 88 per cent of those carers who reported that the person with Parkinson's could not travel alone had been obliged to stop paid employment (Figure 8.1).

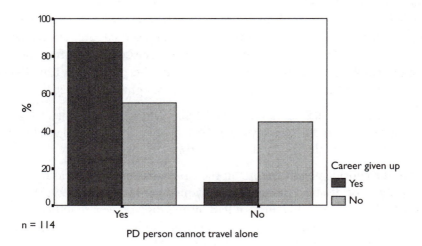

Figure 8.1 Person with Parkinson's unable to travel alone and carer's employment

Personal care

Personal care was another area which illustrated this effect of shared disadvantage and knock-on social and emotional consequences. The need for personal care is frequently a key criterion for eligibility for community health or social care services, and provision of personal care is commonly identified as being at the heart of the 'heavy end' of caring. Over a third of the people with Parkinson's in this community care survey needed a lot of help with personal care at least some of the time. However, 72 per cent were receiving at least some personal care from a partner. Overall, family members were providing significant amounts of personal care. Disturbingly, although 21 per cent of carers reported that they were in poor health and suffered from a chronic condition themselves, the health of the carer made absolutely no difference to the level of care being provided. The following is a particularly stark illustration of how the carer's own difficulties are compounded by her life being inextricably bound up with the disability experienced by the 'main sufferer':

> My mother is 76 and in ill health herself. She is not capable of caring for my father and I feel that she should be offered more assistance. Social Services did put my father to bed at night but they said that it was too much for two women on their own so they withdrew the service leaving a 76-year-old woman with asthma and emphysema to cope on her own.

As with mobility, some surprising connections emerged between severity of physical problems experienced by the person with Parkinson's and the carer experiencing the concomitant social and emotional problems alongside. For example, there was a tendency for people to suffer from depression if they needed high levels of personal care. Inversely, those who did not report depression were less likely to need high levels of personal care. The depression that is associated with needing high levels of personal care often comes hand in hand with feeling that one's dignity has been lost. This can affect both parties in the caring relationship, as this daughter explained:

> My dad can't take her to the toilet, he *won't* take her to the toilet. He gets embarrassed and so does my mum. They're from the old school you know, there's certain things you do on your own territory.

There is a considerable literature on the stress associated with caring for a seriously ill or disabled or ageing family member (Keigher, 1999; Parker, 1990). The data from this study of Parkinson's disease seem to indicate that it is not simply the physical care-giving which induces that stress, but the socioemotional context in which it is given. Thus, care that significantly impacts upon the lifestyle of the carer at the same time as impacting on their physical well-being results in that carer being seriously and disadvantageously affected. In this study, the likelihood of carers reporting stress, depression and related emotional difficulties increased for those giving high levels of personal care, particularly night-time and nursing care. Of those carers who reported that their emotional health had suffered as a result of caring, 51 per cent were giving nursing care and 54 per cent were giving a lot of help with managing and administering medication (Figure 8.2).

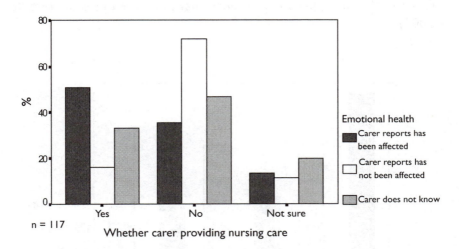

Figure 8.2 Effect of providing nursing care on carer's emotional health

Communication problems

Significant numbers of the people with Parkinson's in both studies experienced a range of communication problems. Communication problems feature high in the accounts of living with a number of disabling conditions, such as motor neurone disease, stroke and dementia. Communicating on behalf of the person with Parkinson's was a major activity for these carers of people with Parkinson's, where the physical limitations imposed by the disease and a socially unaccommodating environment created a situation in which the carer had to act for the person with Parkinson's. Forty-one per cent stated that they had to act as advocate for the person with Parkinson's, 21 per cent saying that this was because other people had difficulty understanding the speech of the person with Parkinson's. Some hidden social effects were uncovered which engendered additional stress for the carers.

Seventy-two per cent gave some to a lot of help with managing finances and 75 per cent with claiming welfare benefits. Giving this sort of help appeared to exacerbate the stress experienced. For example, giving higher levels of help with financial matters correlated with carers saying that their emotional health had been adversely affected by caring (Figure 8.3). Since the majority of the people with Parkinson's was male and the majority of the carers was female, and also spouse carers, it may be that the impact of reversing traditional gender roles in marriage is a factor here. Being forced to change the lifelong pattern in relation to financial management was also found by Argyle, in her study of older carers, to cause role strain (Argyle, 2001).

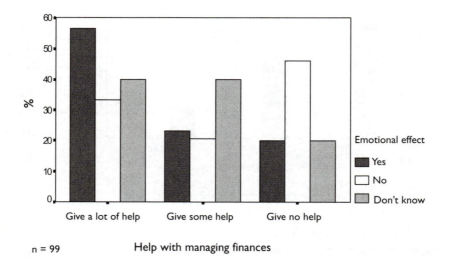

Figure 8.3 Effect of managing finances on carer's emotional well-being

Shared restrictions in social and leisure activities

The effects of the disease on the social and leisure activities of both the people with Parkinson's and their family members were also severe. Sixty-eight per cent of those with Parkinson's disease stated that they were not able to do the things that they wished to do, 62 per cent saying that this was directly due to the physical limitations of their illness. For those who reported *a lot of difficulty* with physical symptoms, high percentages reported both these restrictions (Table 8.1).

Table 8.1 Relationship between severity of symptoms and social life

	Not able to do all things that wish valid (%)	Limited due to physical effects of illness valid (%)	n
Whole sample	68	62	196
Report a lot of difficulty with tremor	82	72	65
Report a lot of difficulty with walking	92	82	88
Report a lot of difficulty with speech	97	93	30
Report a lot of difficulty with swallowing	88	84	25
Report a lot of difficulty with dribbling	90	85	41
Report a lot of difficulty with tiredness	82	77	96
Report a lot of difficulty with bowel or bladder	78	74	49

As in the other examples, the physical limitations stemming directly from the disease result in social restrictions and disadvantage for both the person with the illness and the carer. The emotional impact is also clear. The degree of severity of limitations on social activities for the person with Parkinson's disease directly correlated with carers' reported coping capacity. For those carers who reported that they found it easy to cope, 53 per cent of the people with Parkinson's disease stated that their social activities were limited by the physical effects of the illness, but for those carers who were struggling to cope and did not know if they could carry on, the figure rose to 88 per cent. Carers' own social lives were significantly affected. Forty-six per cent reported that they had had to make changes and 36 per cent stated that they had fewer opportunities to go out. Again, the circular process, in which both the person with Parkinson's disease and the carer were caught up, of severity of physical symptoms, increased levels of care given, significant social limitations and corresponding emotional problems, was demonstrated. Of those carers who reported that they had fewer opportunities to engage in social activities, 55 per cent were giving a lot of personal care and only four per cent were giving no personal care. Sixty-four per cent of those reporting restrictions in their social activities also said that their emotional health had been negatively affected by caring and only 23 per cent said there had been no effect on their emotional health.

Anxiety

A number of studies of Parkinson's disease have highlighted the levels of stress experienced by spouse carers (Calder *et al.*, 1991; Miller *et al.*, 1996). In this community care study, anxiety was a common feature for both people with Parkinson's disease themselves and also their carers. This anxiety was frequently related to fears about physical deterioration in the future (cited by 51%) and feelings of insecurity created by trying to manage the condition in the present. For carers, the main anxiety was their ability to continue caring as they grew older and in the face of declining health themselves. The next most commonly cited fear was concern about the health and well-being of the person with Parkinson's. Thus, the joint and single anxieties of carer and cared for person are interchangeable.

A major impact of Parkinson's disease, which itself is a source of anxiety for both people with Parkinson's disease and their carers, is the 'on–off' pattern of physical symptoms:

> The off periods are rather unpredictable... There is a marked difference in my condition both mentally and physically when the medication is not controlling the symptoms... I find it difficult to achieve the elusive balance with my drugs between not being completely switched on and experiencing the symptoms of an overdose. Choosing between the two states is like asking whether you prefer to be burnt or scalded. (Person with Parkinson's)

This was also linked to the side-effects of drug treatments:

> The side effects were terrible. Hallucinations, confusion. He started getting very aggressive. He didn't recognise me. (Carer)

I had one lot of tablets, I says to my husband, I'm going crackers, it's driving me round the bend. (Person with Parkinson's)

Loneliness, isolation and stigma

These problems contribute to the experience of isolation. Loneliness and isolation were highlighted and commented upon by both the people with Parkinson's disease themselves and by their carers, and linked to both anxiety and depression. Couples might spend all their time together, and hence not experience loneliness, but they still reported a sometimes extreme sense of social isolation. This resulted from the twin effect of being left to manage the illness largely on their own, and of being acutely discomfited by their forays into public life (one woman commented of her husband, 'He doesn't do public'). The stigma experienced by the person with Parkinson's was shared by the family member. This inextricable sharing of the social limitations experienced by the person with Parkinson's and the concomitant emotional problems was explained by one carer:

> I feel less relaxed in other people's company because of my anxiety about my husband's ability to cope with social occasions... I feel depressed by my husband's inability to participate in conversation and other activities in the easy way that he used to. (Carer)

Embarrassment was one of the most disturbing knock-on socioemotional effects of the physical symptoms and it affected both the people with Parkinson's disease and their carers. Thirty-three per cent of the people with Parkinson's disease said that they were embarrassed about their condition in public and therefore tended to shy away from social occasions:

> Parkinson's is not acceptable in company. (Person with Parkinson's)

> I have to refuse invitations to restaurants as I cannot handle cutlery properly. (Person with Parkinson's)

Avoiding embarrassment often led to self-imposed withdrawal, whether in company or from society almost wholesale:

> I soon have trouble trying to talk so I just sit and disappear into the background. Let them talk, talk and just listen. It's best like that. (Person with Parkinson's)

> Other people are unaware of PD problems such as shaking and spilling of food. The PD sufferer tends to lose confidence and is loath to go out, therefore both the sufferer and the carer start to become house-bound. (Carer)

Problems with speech, either other people not understanding the unclear speech of the person with Parkinson's or of them freezing mid-sentence, are a significant source of embarrassment. Family members (wives in particular) find themselves either jumping in to speak on behalf of the person with Parkinson's or holding back for fear of belittling their partner but feeling acutely their frustration and despair. Many respondents in these studies, carers and people with Parkinson's, commented on the disabling and stigmatising effects of the wholesale ignorance about the illness, which they encountered on a daily basis.

Relationship difficulties and sexual problems

Difficulties in close and intimate relationships where one person has a chronic, disabling illness or condition are commonly reported. However, only eight per cent of people with Parkinson's disease in the community care survey reported that they had experienced relationship difficulties as a consequence of their illness. In the qualitative study which followed the progress of 22 people with Parkinson's over a 12-month period, roughly twice as many reported at the end of the period as at the beginning that Parkinson's had reduced the quality of their relationships. Whilst the pre-existing relationship between the person with Parkinson's and the carer is that most obviously affected by the experience of living with the illness, other relationships for both parties were also affected in these studies. For carers particularly, there was a correlation between severity of physical symptoms of the person with Parkinson's (suggesting more intensive caring) and the reporting of adverse effects on their other relationships. For example, those carers who reported a negative effect on their other relationships were significantly more likely to be giving nursing and night-time care. This negative impact often translated into feelings of guilt:

> As soon as he rings up I'll go…and they always think I'm there for hours… I'm torn between everybody. (Carer)

Fourteen per cent of people with Parkinson's disease reported sexual problems stemming from their Parkinson's disease, although this represented 21 per cent of men and only 3 per cent of women. A surprising number of people in the longitudinal qualitative study reported sexual problems at the highest level of difficulty. For those reporting them, sexual problems and sexuality issues often assumed major importance. One man highlighted it thus:

> Problem with Parkinson's is that it affects my sex life, it cuts it right in half sometimes... At the surgery they take it as a big joke, they laugh. I was embarrassed by that – they laughed at me. (Person with Parkinson's)

This insensitive (or perhaps embarrassed) response from service providers, on an issue which was clearly of great significance to the patient, is perhaps one reason why partners in both studies by and large did not comment on sexual problems, despite the known impact of the disease and its drug treatments on sexual function.

Living with Parkinson's disease in old age

I started by highlighting the incidence of Parkinson's disease in older age groups and we should conclude by considering the particular experience of frail and sick older people, many of them cared for by a similarly aged partner with his or her own health problems. Social gerontologists have for two decades or more pointed out the disadvantaged position of older people in Western societies and the stigmatising impact of ageist attitudes which undermine their well-being, quality of life and opportunities. A little-researched feature, however, is the simultaneous disadvantage of ageing with a disability or chronic illness (although see Zarb and Oliver, 1993, for an exception to this). Even less is known about the experience of shared disadvantage which accompanies the lives of older couples living with chronic and serious ill health. The following account captures one couple's experience:

> Over the years she's gradually deteriorated. She can't walk at all now, well, not very much outside...the inconvenience of it is getting more acute...she needs constant attendance really. I help her dress and undress. I do the cooking, the ironing and the washing. When you get older the worries seem to get worse, but we roll along... (Husband of 77-year-old woman with Parkinson's disease)

These studies of Parkinson's disease paint a picture of shared hardship and marginalisation. In the community care study the oldest person with Parkinson's was 91 and the oldest carer 81. The female Parkinsonians tended to be older than the men, but male carers tended to be older than the women, suggesting a pattern of spouse caring. Ninety-seven per cent of carers over the age of 65 identified themselves as the partner of the person with Parkinson's. Of these older carers, four were also caring for grandchildren, but 92 per cent said there was no one else living in the household. Fifty-three per cent said they were the only regular carer (formal or informal) and only 9 per cent said caring was shared with other members of the family. Fifteen per cent said they had had no visits from relatives in the last month and 31 per cent had had five visits or fewer. Given the targeting of frail older people in community care guidance and health and social care eligibility criteria, it might have been hoped that the data for older couples would have shown comparatively higher levels of formal service provision and lower levels of unmet need. Regrettably, this was not the case, a picture emerging instead in which the escalating impact of the disease was compounded by problems associated with both the physical effects of old age and ageism in terms of service provision.

Mobility problems presented particular difficulties for the older couple. The following scenario, where the husband's poor health prevented him pushing the wheelchair for long distances and was the reason given by the couple for them becoming socially isolated, was not untypical:

> With his heart being the way it is he can't honestly push me very far because he starts getting angina pains and he has bronchial asthma and then he's gasping for breath.

Holidays, often a very important part of life for couples once they have retired from work, were severely affected. Only 56 per cent of carers over 65 reported that they went on holiday, of whom 94 per cent did so with the person they cared for. Going on holiday was very much linked to the levels of care being provided; 77 per cent of those who did not go away were involved in night-time care and 48 per cent in nursing care.

Ageism operating in relation to service provision was felt very keenly by some of these carers. A number complained that the services offered were entirely inappropriate, due to the fact that the person over 65 who has Parkinson's is seen as 'old' first and foremost:

> There's no way he would go in a home, that'd be the last. He's always said 'I don't want to be with old people'. I mean he's 70 in February but he's not like a 70-year-old.

> He is 66 but he is a young 66... I know the lady next door and her dad used to go in for respite but he was 90. When you think of a 66-year-old lying in bed next to someone who is 90.

It was these factors which provoked feelings of guilt for older carers. Their expressions of guilt related to accepting help which they felt went against the wishes or best interests of the person they cared for:

> I felt very guilty putting him in hospital because I know he hates it and I felt guilty about having a bit of free time.

Conclusion

These studies of Parkinson's disease show an intricate pattern of family members caught up in a spiralling impact of sharing their lives with someone who has a serious, debilitating illness, misunderstood by the general public and even some service providers. This spiralling effect stems from the physical symptoms but becomes all-pervasive in its effects on the lives of the people with Parkinson's and those closely associated with them. Thus, the more severe and less controlled the physical symptoms, the greater the impact on the practicalities of everyday life, with corresponding knock-on negative effects in social relations generally and emotional well-being. Family members acting as carers become particularly caught up. In these studies, those who reported the greatest degree of stress and damage to their own physical and mental health were those who were heavily involved in giving personal, nursing and night-time care. A major source of stress and reason for the decrease in their quality of life arose from experiencing the disadvantage and stigma alongside the person with Parkinson's. The significance of this aspect is reflected by the Parkinson's Disease Society UK in their holding of an annual Parkinson's Awareness Week.

These people with Parkinson's disease and their family members provide us with a particularly sharp example of the disadvantage and stigma experienced by those who share the lives of the person with chronic, debilitating illness. Their experiences will resonate with others. As service providers, we may reflect how little some of our practice with people with chronic illness is underpinned by the social model of disability, as we effectively confine management of the 'problem' to the person with the illness and their immediate family members. Thus we isolate, disadvantage and stigmatise those on whom it impacts in their daily lives. We need to be reminded that the negative connotations of 'disability by association' are also socially created. This carer, whose wife had recently been admitted to nursing home care because of the severity of her illness, poignantly indicated the way in which that association could be otherwise constructed:

> I'd rather have her here, that's the truth. It's such a minus. Physically, I'm better off, but not when we're talking of quality. No, I wouldn't think so, just watching television.

Note

1   Formerly Lloyd.

References

Anderson, R. and Bury, M. (eds) (1988) *Living with Chronic Illness: The Experience of Patients and their Families.* London: Unwin Hyman.

Argyle, E. (2001) 'Poverty, disability and the role of older carers.' *Disability and Society 16,* 4, 585–95.

Bury, M. (1997) *Health and Illness in a Changing Society.* London: Routledge.

Calder, S.A., Ebmeier, K.P., Stewart, L., Crawford, J.R. and Besson, J.A.O. (1991) 'The prediction of stress in carers: the role of behaviour, reported self-care and dementia in patients with idiopathic Parkinson's disease.' *International Journal of Geriatric Psychiatry 6,* 737–42.

Davey, B. and Seale, C. (eds) (1996) *Experiencing and Explaining Disease.* Buckingham: OUP.

Holloway, M. (2006) 'Traversing the network: a user-led care pathway approach to the management of Parkinson's disease in the community.' *Health and Social Care in the Community 14,* 1, 63–73.

Keigher, S. (1999) 'Feminist Issues from the Gray Market in Personal Care for the Elderly.' In S.M. Neysmith (ed.) *Critical Issues for Future Social Work Practice with Aging Persons.* New York: Columbia University Presss, pp.155–86.

Lloyd, M. (1999) 'The New Community Care for People with Parkinson's Disease and their Carers.' In R. Percival and P. Hobson (eds) *Parkinson's Disease: Studies in Psychological and Social Care.* Leicester: BPS Books.

Lloyd, M. (2000) 'Where has all the care management gone? The challenge of Parkinson's disease to the health and social care interface.' *British Journal of Social Work 30,* 737–54.

Lloyd, M. (2002) *The Patient-Led Care Pathway Approach: Report on 'Development and Implementation of an Information Pack and Patient-Led Needs Monitoring Form for the Management of Parkinson's Disease in the Community'.* Final project report to the Welfare Research Committee of the Parkinson's Disease Society UK.

Lloyd, M. and Smith, M. (1998) *Assessment and Service Provision under the New Community Care Arrangements for People with Parkinson's Disease and their Carers.* arc Research Reports No. 13. Manchester: University of Manchester.

Locker, D. (1983) *Disability and Disadvantage: The Consequences of Chronic Illness.* London: Tavistock.

Meara, J. and Hobson, P. (2000) 'The Epidemiology of Parkinson's Disease and Parkinsonism in Elderly Subjects.' In J. Meara and W. Koller (eds) *Parkinson's Disease and Parkinsonism in the Elderly.* Cambridge: Cambridge University Press.

Miller, E., Berrios, G.E., Politynska, B.E. (1996) 'Caring for someone with Parkinson's disease: factors that contribute to distress.' *International Journal of Geriatric Psychiatry 11,* 263–68.

Oliver, M. and Barnes, C. (1998) *Disabled People and Social Policy: From Exclusion to Inclusion.* London: Longman.

Oliver, M. and Sapey, B. (1999) *The Social Model of Disability.* Basingstoke: Macmillan.

Parker, G. (1990) *With Due Care and Attention: A Review of Research on Informal Care.* London: Family Policy Studies Centre.

Radley, A. (ed.) (1993) *Worlds of Illness: Biographical and Cultural Perspectives on Health and Disease.* London: Routledge.

Scambler, G. and Higgs, P. (eds) (1998) *Modernity, Medicine and Health.* London: Routledge.

Walker, A. and Townsend, P. (1981) (eds) *Disability in Britain: A Manifesto of Rights.* Oxford: Martin Robertson.

Walmsley, J., Reynolds, J., Shakespeare, P. and Woolfe, R. (1992) *Health, Welfare and Practice: Reflecting on Roles and Relationships.* London: Sage. Available at www.parkinsons.org.uk (accessed 31 January 2006).

Yarrow, S. (1999) 'Members' 1998 Survey of the Parkinson's Disease Society of the United Kingdom.' In R. Percival and P. Hobson (eds) *Parkinson's Disease: Studies in Psychological and Social Care.* Leicester: BPS Books.

Zarb, G. and Oliver, M. (1993) *Ageing with a Disability: What do They Expect after all these Years?* London: University of Greenwich.

Chapter 9

Social Work, Disadvantage by Association and Anti-Oppressive Practice

Jonathan Parker

Social work is a values-based profession and can never be neutral (see Beckett and Maynard, 2005). It must be so given that:

> Social workers deal with some of the most vulnerable people in our society at times of greatest stress. There can be tragic consequences if things go wrong. Social workers often get a bad press. What they do not get is day to day coverage of the work they do to protect and provide for some of the most vulnerable people in our society. (Department of Health, 2002: i)

In their work with people, social workers make decisions that may have far-reaching consequences for their lives and this must be done according to transparent, understandable principles. These requirements may be open to challenge, debate and contest and often they are. The value base of social work has often brought it into conflict with those in positions of power. Indeed, the promotion of a values-based perspective has provided ammunition to those who wish to discredit it. The association of social work with values of respect, acceptance and the promotion of inclusive social justice means that social workers are seen as holding beliefs which are out of step with popular thinking and this can be employed against them. In the 1990s, for instance, the success of social work in promoting anti-oppressive practice led to an assault against social work using the term 'political correctness' pejoratively to dilute the challenge of anti-oppressive practice in countering the impact of disadvantage, discrimination and oppression and to belittle the processes of social work within wider society. Indeed,

Dominelli (2004) believes these attacks have led to a shift in which employers now hold power over academics and have consolidated control over practitioners, favouring a technical, bureaucratic approach to the 'management' of vulnerable and marginalised people. This chapter will outline a theoretical approach to disadvantage and stigma in contemporary social work and social care. This will be followed by an exploration of social work in the context of anti-oppressive practice as an organising framework in contemporary social work. The association of social workers with the marginalised, disempowered and disadvantaged in society will be considered as one of the ways in which social workers themselves assume the perceived negativities of those with whom they work. A model for social work practice based around anti-oppressive values will be presented.

Theoretical orientation

Examining the contexts of disadvantage by association (see Chapter 1), we can discern situational, structural and social factors that have an impact on the ways social work is perceived, perceives itself and therefore practises. Looking at the situational perspective, we know that social work offices located in patches, that is, in the areas served, are often positioned in areas of deprivation, in dilapidated buildings that are unattractive and uninviting. Not only does this construct a view that the disadvantage and marginalisation experienced by those using the service is justified and that they are, indeed, 'worthless' or 'worth less' than others; it also constructs a similar view for the social workers within those offices. In their own eyes, their value and treatment is equated with the negative assumptions and popularly accepted stereotypes concerning the people they serve which may lead to a number of possible reactions, including identification with service users and resistance against the perceived abuses of power (Foucault, 1977, 1981). On the other hand, such associations may lead to a 'distancing and demarcation', an 'us-and-them' approach (Parker, 2005a), in which popular negative perceptions of service users are assimilated and a controlling, regulatory approach to social work is reinforced. This, in turn, produces a nugatory conceptualisation of social work in dealing with the 'undeserving' which, in itself, becomes self-defeating. However, both perspectives allow the concept of disadvantage by association. By resisting alongside service users popular stereotypes may be confirmed. By distancing themselves from service users, social workers are themselves engaging in the process of disadvantaging others by associating them with elements of disadvantage and marginalisation rather than analysing and challenging its causes. If we employ Bourdieu's analysis of *habitus* as those dispositions which structure what we do at the level of everyday practice (Bourdieu, 1977), we might understand that the internalisation of externally held 'common-sense' understandings may create a wider, albeit unconscious, view amongst social work agencies and policy-makers that social workers can legitimately be treated unfairly (see Bourdieu, 1996), further confirming their low worth and esteem and those of service users.

Some social services offices, of course, have been so distanced from service users that an assumed moral and value distance is promoted which structures 'common-sense' thinking amongst social workers, managers and the wider public including service users themselves. Also, as organisational changes take place within social work, health care and the public services, practitioners are no longer working in uniprofessional local authority team settings as the norm (Quinney, 2006). Indeed, a range of changing practices are developing including working as the sole social worker within a wider multidisciplinary team. The positioning of the social worker within these teams is often an indicator of the views others have of not only the social work role and task but the users of services. There are no easy answers to situational disadvantage and, indeed, it is the case that social workers seek to identify with those with whom they work in respect of naming the injustice and marginalisation experienced. However, it is important that social workers examine situational factors and challenge the negative constructions that often emanate and are accepted uncritically.

In structural terms, we can see that the importance and profile of social work, since the coming to power of the Labour Government in 1997, has been raised considerably. This is seen in the continuing Department of Health campaign to attract social work students and practitioners into the profession (Department of Health, undated), the development of the new qualifying awards throughout the UK (Parker, 2005b) and the increased expenditure on public services (CSCI, 2005). To some extent, social work is experiencing its 'Macmillan moment' in that we have 'never had it so good'. However, this is not the whole story, and social work is conceptualised in a way that seeks to maximise the contribution of people to the existing systems, that seeks to cut waste and to target, punitively, those it associates with some kind of social deviance, whether being out of work, living in unconventional communities or struggling with living situations. There has also developed a degree of anti-intellectualism which understands social work solely as a practical venture but not one in which the critical application of considered theoretical models is of any importance (Parker, 2007). There is a lack of emphasis on research for and into social work practice, which is effectively curtailed further by the increase in delivery time associated with many qualifying programmes despite the growing acknowledgement of social work as a potentially burgeoning research discipline by such august bodies as the Economic and Social Research Council (Shaw, Arksey and Mullender, 2004). There is a further privileging of the employer perspective in respect of education at qualifying and post-qualifying levels, which has, in practice, marginalised higher education perspectives, as suggested by Dominelli (2004). This, in effect, may neglect the improvement in quality of practitioner thinking and critical skills to such an extent that service user needs and ultimately service needs are neglected, although there is renewed emphasis on lifelong learning and continual updating by the introduction of a new post-qualifying framework. However, these movements serve the interests of those who control the terms of the debate. Learning is for practice sanctioned by those with power whilst critical education is marginalised. This represents a microcosm of perceived attacks on higher education and the independence of learning and scholarship.

It is evident that those who use social work services are often shunned and stigmatised by society. As Payne (2005: 2) points out:

> Most societies' values assume that people will manage their difficulties and fulfil their potential without help outside their family or local community. People calling on professional social work, therefore, are often stigmatised for needing help, adding to their already marginalised status in their society.

He points out further that in the early days of social work, stigma was employed as a method of encouraging change, whilst contemporary social work practice more often seeks to challenge such attitudes and promote self-help. Social factors perhaps most clearly reflect the disadvantage by association experienced by social workers. The negative image in which the public see social work is well known. Indeed, in research into the state of the social work and social care profession, Eborall and Gamerson (2001) identified that one of the key reasons dissuading people from entering the profession was its negative image. Social factors further reflecting this negativity are found in popular jokes about social workers and light bulbs, and in claiming to be part of a different and perhaps more onerous profession. On a more serious note, however, it is still social workers who tend to be pilloried for failures in care or tragedies that occur, often in a multi-disciplinary context (Stanley and Manthorpe, 2004). Other disciplines are not disadvantaged because social work is associated in the minds of commentators and in popular mythology with the value systems and beliefs that allow such mistakes to be made.

Social workers are disadvantaged by association with the people they work with because of the ways in which people are assigned to distinct binary groups – good and bad; deserving and undeserving; rich and poor;

favoured and unfavoured; genuine and bogus and so on. The process by which this disadvantage comes about can be understood in Bourdesian terms in which social work and social workers are both *structured structures,* in positions that are socially constructed by negative assumptions and *structuring structures,* in which position and action influences and creates some of the objective social categories from which social work is socially constructed (Bourdieu, 1996). This bi-directionality of constructing and constructed allows social workers to challenge disadvantage at a range of levels, including social work and its personnel, the people with whom it works, and popular social assumptions. It is within the context of anti-oppressive practice that social workers can begin this process of resistance.

What is anti-oppressive practice?

When considering stigma and disadvantage a Foucauldian analysis of power is useful. Power relations are more complex than a perspective which suggests there are those who have power and wield it over others and those who do not. Power is exercised within relations between people and even those whom might be believed to be the most 'powerless' resist and exert their own power within the context of human relations. This understanding is central to understanding anti-oppressive practice in social work and the exercise of power by those who are disadvantaged and those disadvantaged by association – the social workers. It is this resistance which has been instrumental in developing the voice and power of service users, who, when seen as experts because of their experiences[1] and self-knowledge should impact on work in a profound and epiphanic way (Wilson and Beresford, 2000). In developing a model to counter disadvantage based on anti-oppressive practice it is important to remember that social workers must take their lead from service users even when acting against the self-determined actions of service users. What this means is not to be neutered or prevented from acting in ways in which social workers are required to act but to seek the views, preferences and wishes of individuals, to seek to understand the narrative perspectives of service users and to stand with them providing opportunities to resolve complex issues and challenge oppressive structures, disadvantage and marginalisation that are often in the development of problematic situations and events. Much of what follows extends the debate begun in Parker (2004).

Anti-oppressive practice is the cornerstone of ethical social work practice. It is relational and emphasises the individual's interactions with the political spheres of social life. It is, however, a much maligned and misunderstood concept and approach to social work. First, we will need to define the terms before exploring some of the implications for practice and for understanding social work's status as disadvantaged by association and the subsequent dangers associated with such an analysis.

There is considerable confusion amongst social workers as to the meaning of anti-discriminatory and anti-oppressive practice. It is often asked whether the two are the same or have different and specific definitions. Thompson (1997: 33) uses the term 'anti-discriminatory practice', describing it as follows:

> An approach to social work practice which seeks to reduce, undermine or eliminate discrimination or oppression specifically in terms of challenging sexism, racism, ageism and disablism... and other forms of discrimination or oppression encountered in social work. Social workers occupy positions of power and influence, and there is considerable scope for discrimination and oppression, whether this is intentional or by default. Anti-discriminatory practice is an attempt to eradicate discrimination and oppression from our own practice and challenge them in the practice of others and in the institutional structures in which we operate. In this respect it is a form of emancipatory practice.

This quotation suggests that the two terms are interchangeable. However, Dalrymple and Burke (1995) warn against this assumption. They state that *anti-discriminatory practice* relates to specific challenges to certain forms of discrimination, often using legislation. An example here might relate to the ways in which the Disability Discrimination Act 1995 might be used to challenge a decision not to make reasonable adjustments to accommodate an employee who declares a disability. *Anti-oppressive practice*, on the other hand, is taken to address wider structural issues and inequalities such as the way the worlds of work and schooling seem to favour the maintenance of different male and female roles.

The debate is not simply a semantic one and may be seen as having far-reaching effects on our understanding of discrimination and oppression and, indeed, the experience of disadvantage by association as social workers. If you favour working solely in an anti-discriminatory way, tackling the impact of a particular form of discrimination resulting from age, gender, race and ethnicity, health status, ability or disability and so on, but ignore the impact of structural and social policy factors, you may begin to rank in order of assumed importance or impact the different forms of discrimination. A hierarchy of oppression may be created in which polarised views become entrenched and certain forms of discrimination are considered worse, or more severe than others (McDonald and Coleman, 1999). This is a useful tool for those who do not wish to see change and have something to gain or protect from preserving their advantaged position. It has the potential to set one group against another without addressing core issues. Of course, this does not mean that social workers should not seek to work in an anti-discriminatory way. It is important and central to learning in practice to challenge the focused abuse of power and exploitation of others using specific legislation, where available, and to consider the particular disadvantages resulting from a specific social division or difference. Anti-discriminatory approaches highlight disadvantage by association experienced by people with whom social workers practise as the discrimination is directly related to the particular characteristics identified within the legislation. It is not peculiar to social work and its operations and applies across all sections and people within society. An anti-oppressive approach is more encompassing.

Some models of anti-oppressive practice

It is fundamental to set oppression and discrimination in a much wider perspective, understanding that oppression is experienced by individuals, groups and communities in diverse ways but from similar interacting elements. These elements include personal prejudices, but not exclusively so, that inform and are informed by the cultures of work and community in which people live, which interact with social factors to maintain the position of those in privileged locations in society. This is reflected in Thompson's PCS model of oppression (see Figure 9.1, also Chapter 1) in which oppression acts as the constructor of personal, cultural and societal views and is constructed, reinforced and revised by them as they interact and permeate the interstices of each level.

The concept suggests, for example, that personal prejudice alone does not explain racism. It is part of it and we may all have examples of racially prejudicial comments that we have found offensive. However, personal prejudice feeds into and from the setting in which it develops; the environment and neighbourhood in which it is found and within the schools, agencies and community groups within a particular location. In turn, the way that society is set up and runs informs how the environment operates and forms yet another influential factor in how discrimination and oppression on racial grounds develops. The personal, cultural and social aspects of life interact to create and recreate patterns of discrimination and oppression. It is important as a social worker undertaking to understand this within the context of the agency in which you are working. The Bourdieusian approach to daily practices introduced earlier may also be applied to anti-oppressive practice which sees the actions and beliefs of the individual,

Personal

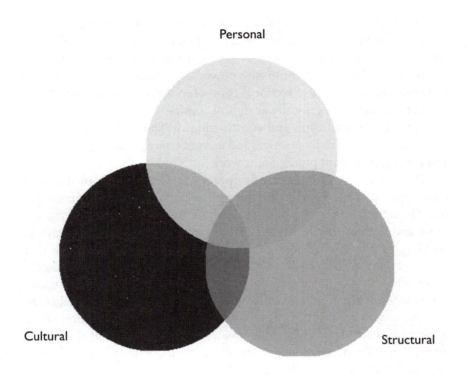

Cultural

Structural

Figure 9.1 Thompson's PCS model of oppression

group or community being influenced by and influencing the structures in which those practices take place. In a similar process to the beliefs of others about social work being influenced by negative social portrayals, stereotypes and structures and those perceptions impacting on the development of social policy and welfare, so too is anti-oppressive practice influenced by and influences social workers who associate with people who are disadvantaged and marginalised.

A social worker practising in a particularly disadvantaged area with high rates of crime, violence, family breakdown, unemployment and disease may empathise with the people with whom he or she works. Because of this, the social worker may assume, in the eyes of others, the mantle of disadvantage experienced by service users. By working with a violent drug user it may be assumed that the social worker is condoning these behaviours and seeking to promote them amongst wider society. It may be that the social worker, on the other hand, is attempting to control and regulate the behaviour of the service user in an attempt to develop conformity to a preconceived norm, seeing the person as associated with disadvantage by area and action. Alternatively, the service user may perceive the social worker as part of an overarching conspiracy of a powerful and elite social group; in a different way seeing the social worker as disadvantaged by association with those with power. Disadvantage by association is a multilayered and multi-directional concept in social work and one that is useful in promoting a critically analytical approach to social situations that identifies the construction and constructing of 'common-sense' assumptions that impact on daily practices and ways of conceptualising social work and those with whom practitioners work.

Dominelli (2002) understands oppression as a continuum that runs from oppression and exploitation through to empowerment and emancipation. Before reaching such a positive outcome, those who are oppressed will resist and it is in this resistance that social workers can be effective in enabling people to challenge, campaign and change. In order to do this, social workers need to understand that oppression takes place within the social arena, and is (re)created by interactions between people in society. Social workers are important in working with people to reduce and eradicate oppression because they work with people in context. However, social workers are part of society and are involved in the interactions that create, recreate or resist oppression and, therefore, need continually to reflect on their position. As Dominelli (2002: 36) states:

> Anti-oppressive practice addresses the whole person and enables a practitioner to relate to his or her client's social context in a way that takes account of the 'allocative and authoritative resources' that both the practitioner and the client bring to the relationship. Thus, anti-oppressive practice takes on board personal, institutional, cultural and economic issues and examines how these impinge on individuals' behaviour and opportunities to develop their full potential as persons living within collective entities.

A mystique has grown up around the terms which has led some social workers not to question or challenge thinking and actions in a critical and reflective way for fear of appearing oppressive or discriminatory. This can lead to the very situation anti-oppressive and anti-discriminatory practice seek to reduce or eradicate. It is important for social workers to question why things are the way they are, the impact this has on practice, on agency ethos and on the people with whom social workers practise.

As a model, anti-oppressive practice provides a way of conceptualising and working with people in a critical and ethical manner, taking issue with popular assumptions and beliefs. Where social workers experience disadvantage by association, the model offers a way of constructing a challenge to the underlying perceptions and assumptions made about the people with whom they are identified. This model requires social workers to examine their own beliefs and assumptions, those of their agencies and wider society and can be extended by agencies and social work supervisors to examine why these associations are made. Practising anti-oppressively is not easy, however.

Anti-oppressive practice is also associated in popular thought with popular and pejorative versions of political correctness as we have seen earlier. This creates a conceptual, theoretical and practice base against which social workers can be judged and which may push them into socially constructed positions of disadvantage. This allows social workers to grasp their social justice mission which is increasingly important as state social work moves towards an increasingly technical-bureaucratic and managerialist function.

Anti-oppressive practice is multidimensional. It is practice that requires social workers to act in ways that first do not oppress and ultimately empower. It is also practice that seeks to change systems that uphold the status quo at the expense of service users, carers, people disadvantaged or marginalised because of social divisions, statuses and socially ascribed roles and attributes. A semantic issue arises with the term anti-oppressive practice in respect of its negative prefix. However, whilst challenge and struggle are important aspects of acting anti-oppressively, the objective is to establish non-oppressive social work practices and eliminate oppression in the lives of service users or, as a preferred term, those who are 'expert by experience'.

The question that must be asked is 'How might an anti-oppressive practice framework be understood in practice?' There are three analytic frameworks that can be applied to our understanding of the development and entrenchment of disadvantage by association in social work:

- economic analysis
- moral analysis
- social justice analysis.

An economic analysis sees service users as vulnerable and marginalised and as such often economically unproductive. Therefore it is assumed either that those people who work alongside them as social workers are there to encourage social engagement and productivity and their actions are judged by the results of that framework, or that social workers too are part of that sector of society that encourage and are too soft on the feckless. Because service users draw on resources and public funds and do not contribute, those who help them should not have greater resource to waste. This economic analysis has permeated social work throughout its history and its development (Payne, 2005). A moral analysis is similar in many ways and develops the economic argument, focuses on moral rectitude and culpability issue in respect of service users rather than productivity. This analysis questions whether service users are worth the effort or whether they are morally bankrupt and natural recidivists by virtue of which they render those who work with them moral outcasts by assisting and supporting them. However, a social justice analysis can also be applied; this interweaves with anti-oppressive practice as a model for challenging the disadvantage experienced by service users whilst employing disadvantage by association experienced by social workers as a means of highlighting and challenging injustice. Social work is about social change and human justice. Social workers sit alongside the marginalised for political as well as interpersonal helping reasons and seek to change existing structures to be more inclusive and supportive. Thus social work is associated with often unpopular and marginalised views and groups. These negative images and perceptions of social work can be reclaimed as a positive approach to dealing with disadvantage by association and championing social justice for all.

Note

1 Acknowledgement to Professor Michael Preston-Shoot for alerting me to this concept.

References

Beckett, C. and Maynard, A. (2005) *Values and Ethics in Social Work.* London: Sage.

Bourdieu, P. (1977) *Outline of a Theory of Practice.* Cambridge: Cambridge University Press.

Bourdieu, P. (1996) 'On the family as a realized category.' *Theory, Culture and Society 13*, 19–26.

CSCI (2005) *State of Social Care in England 2004–05.* Available at www.csci.org.uk/about_csci/ publications/the_state_of_social_care_in_en.aspx (accessed January 2006).

Dalrymple, J. and Burke, B. (1995) *Anti-Oppressive Practice: Social Care and the Law.* Buckingham: Open University Press.

Department of Health (2002) *Requirements for the Training of Social Workers.* London: Department of Health.

Department of Health (undated) Social Work Recruitment Campaign Site. Available at http://207.45.112.173/ (accessed January 2006).

Dominelli, L. (2002) *Anti-Oppressive Social Work Theory and Practice.* Basingstoke: Palgrave.

Dominelli, L. (2004) *Social Work: Theory and Practice for a Changing Profession.* Cambridge: Polity Press.

Eborall, C. and Gamerson, K. (2001) *Desk Research on Recruitment and Retention in Social Care and Social Work.* London: Prepared for COI Communications for the Department of Health.

Foucault, M. (1977) *Discipline and Punish: The Birth of the Prison.* London: Penguin.

Foucault, M. (1981) *History of Sexuality, Volume 1 An Introduction.* Harmondsworth: Penguin.

McDonald, P. and Coleman, M. (1999) 'Deconstructing hierarchies of oppression and adopting a "multiple model" approach to anti-oppressive practice.' *Social Work Education 18*, 1, 19–33.

Parker, J. (2004) *Effective Practice Learning in Social Work.* Exeter: Learning Matters.

Parker, J. (2005a) 'Constructing dementia and dementia care: daily practices in a day care setting.' *Journal of Social Work 5*, 3, 261–78.

Parker, J. (2005b) 'Developing perceptions of competence during practice learning.' *British Journal of Social Work*. Available at http://bjsw.oxfordjournals.org/cgi/reprint/bch347?ij-key=j0v3DZdwH3NvcHZ&keytype=ref (accessed October 2005).

Parker, J. (2007) 'The Process of Social Work: Assessment, Planning, Intervention and Review.' In M. Lymbery and K. Postle (eds) *Social Work. A Companion to Learning*. London: Sage.

Payne, M. (2005) *The Origins of Social Work: Continuity and Change*. Basingstoke: Palgrave.

Quinney, A. (2006) *Collaboration in Social Work Practice*. Exeter: Learning Matters.

Shaw, I., Arksey, H. and Mullender, A. (2004) *ESRC Research, Social Work and Social Care*. London: Social Care Institute for Excellence.

Stanley, N. and Manthorpe, J. (eds) (2004) *The Age of the Inquiry*. London: Routledge.

Thompson, N. (1997) *Anti-Discriminatory Practice*. 2nd edition. Basingstoke: Macmillan.

Wilson, A. and Beresford, P. (2000) 'Anti-oppressive practice: emancipation or appropriation.' *British Journal of Social Work 30*, 5, 553–73.

Chapter 10

Disadvantage as an Associative Concept; Reflections and Some Further Considerations

Peter Burke

This chapter draws together a unifying framework to enable an appreciation of how disadvantage by association might inform practice, given the analysis and examination within the preceding chapters. In doing so common elements from the differing perspectives offered in Chapters 2 to 9 will first be considered, including reflection on the findings and discussion areas raised. It is evident that social work practice needs to identify and challenge the experience of associative disadvantage and, in the process, to build a working relationship with service users, define a role for social workers and make a difference to the experience of stigma-creating situations.

The common theme articulated in this work is that disadvantage is demonstrable. The areas covered include the looked after system for children, the siblings of children with disabilities, the experience of families where there is a drug user, working individuals and families affected by HIV/AIDS, issues of sexuality in an ageing population, the construction of dementia, the experience of living with Parkinson's disease, and disadvantage in anti-oppressive practice in the field of social work. There is no intention to suggest that this coverage of varied user groups is in any sense complete, only that the concept under examination is borne out by the material examined from ranging sources.

Extending beyond the scope of this book, associative disadvantage may also be linked to families of young and adult offenders, vulnerable adults, the ageing population, the homeless, those in transitional arrangements, social isolation and varied geographical locations; indeed, any number of situations or conditions influencing community life. Such is the diversity of disadvantage that all possibilities are not and cannot be covered, although this book will assist that consideration. Clearly, the need to extend and make an examination of a further range of client and user situations is warranted, but given the broad-brush approach that has been adopted here, some unification of practice-related matters is needed and is, nevertheless, possible. The evidence produced in the chapters is not subject to a full review, for that is not the purpose here; rather it is to clarify the common factors, where they exist, within each of the chapters in an effort to aid our understanding of disadvantage, and associative conditions relating to stigma. This is not a short-cut to the earlier material which needs to be considered within its own context; it accepts the evidence presented to move that examination forward.

What are the common elements that underpin practice, accepting that associative conditions are real for the user groups examined, for their families and for the workers involved? First, what have we learned?

Essentials
The essence of associative disadvantage is stigma through contact with groups or individuals already stigmatised in some way, whether through disability, condition or situation. The impact is as simple as a ripple effect in a pool of water. At the centre of the ripple is the difference or problem experienced by the individual. That individual or person is in some way, due to their situation, socially excluded, isolated or shunned by others. The social model of disability suggests that disability is created by interactions with society, which constructs disability beyond a level that any impairment might promote, indicate or remotely suggest. In a similar way the creation of associative orders of disadvantage, like that of disability, the imposition of stigma, which is unlike the experience of physical pain, is not actual or real, but created by others to distance one individual or group from an identity with another.

The creation of a stigmatised other radiates through an associative order to engulf those closest to the individual, including siblings, family and relatives and indeed workers in direct contact with the originating source: it is the ripple effect of associative disadvantage (see Figure 10.1).

It appears very clearly that the way in which we react to undesirable situations, those stigmatised as different, is to avoid confrontation. Anyone close to a possibly stigmatised individual or group might therefore risk some threat or fear, and therefore would do better to avoid them. Figure 10.1 indicates that the association of disadvantage is sufficient to cause a degree of fear and consequently the individual, the family; those outside the

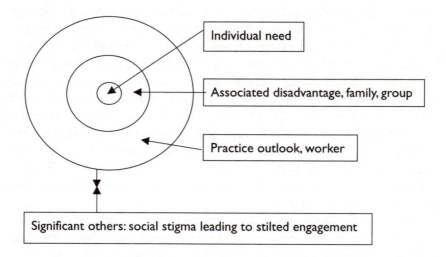

Figure 10.1 Circle of influence: Stigma, associative disadvantage and practice relationships

immediate circle of influence might view even the worker with some uncertainty. In Figure 10.1 the avoidance or stigmatising effect is indicated by the box for significant others, those who seek to avoid contact with those considered disadvantaged. The sense of disadvantage emanates from the individual to include the family, and may also include the worker, as illustrated in the case of those working with HIV/AIDS (Chapter 5).

Dominelli (1997: 37) discussed reactive behaviours in her examination of the colour-blind approach to racism. A social worker expressed the following view: 'I treat black people and white people the same. We are all members of the human race. There are no differences between people for me'. This view seems to be offered by someone who might feel liberal in his or her attitudes and even freethinking, but Dominelli is very persuasive in saying that this is not the case. Dominelli explains that treating all people as the same is being justified on the grounds of treating all people equally. However, this fails to acknowledge the structural inequalities faced by black people. Ignoring difference provides a 'colour-blind' view of the reality. Interestingly, Holdsworth (1991) proffers equality as underpinning her theory, but this is related to treating people with disabilities as people having the right to make choices. So, extending that analogy to the social model of disability, the concept of equality would suggest that to treat all disabled people as the same as non-disabled people would exclude their difference; the reality is that needs, difference and diversity should be recognised, acknowledged and acted upon. We cannot all do the same things or go to the same places if access is not provided and when mobility problems make access difficult: we are not all the same and it is a fallacious argument to suggest otherwise.

It is much the same line of reasoning, I would argue, that claims that to ignore the impact of associative conditions would also lead to a 'colour-blind' perspective because that means we fail to deal with issues of access, attitudes and the individual needs of people subject to stigmatisation. Disadvantaged and stigmatised people are not all the same, hence my examination of situation, structural and social aspects of stigma in Chapter 1 to demonstrate how difference may be conceptualised in associative conditions.

Having reaffirmed that associative conditions exist, which the preceding chapters identify within a set of varying and ranging situations, to ignore them is a failure to recognise the needs of individuals who are disadvantaged in this way. It is helpful, and indeed necessary, to consider how the challenge of rebalancing the inequality that such disadvantage brings, and that is a factor that is central to the intent behind this concluding discussion. It is important that any implications for practice, given the range of clients and service users who form the hub of this examination, are summarised, and I shall do so in the next part of this chapter.

Practice implications

In social work practice, and in child care particularly, then the centrality of the child in need is foremost. This is illustrated by the *Framework for Assessment* (Department of Health, 2000), where the need for an ecological assessment with its domains of child development, parenting capacity and family and environmental factors should be familiar to most practitioners, even those with limited experience. Indeed, my research (Burke and Montgomery, 2003) indicated that problems with the framework required a further domain concerned with siblings, which otherwise seem relegated within a more general sense to family and environment factors, seemingly like an 'others' category. Criticisms of the framework (see Garrett, 2003; Houston, 2002; Powell, 2001) seem to indicate that the framework is partial in its application due to the scale of what is considered ecological. It seems that the framework is at the same time too broad and too narrow, such that it cannot be used as an objective instrument. Indeed, the triangular representation of the assessment framework is too limiting and selective in the assessment process (Donald and Jureidini, 2004) with its independent domains, so ecological assessments (Jack, 1997) need more of a systems framework, as shown in Figure 10.1, which is centrally linked to the individual with disadvantage permeating the differing layers of social interaction.

Perhaps associative disadvantage represents one way of unscrambling the disjunction of the trivariate format that any competent and comprehensive assessment, applied in practice, will reveal.

In identifying a way through the assessment framework, rather than using the assessment triangle with its complexity of assessment requirements, we reconceptualise the framework with its three identifiable domains – of child developmental needs, parenting capacity and family and environmental factors – into a ripple effect model of associative disadvantage, shown as Figure 10.1. This model contained all the variable interactions within the social ordering of the individual identified as having a particular need, problem or difficulty, retaining the centrality of the individual or, in the example of the framework, the child.

Possible consequences

The sense of disadvantage affects initially the individual at the centre of the circle, then the carers, parents or family, before reaching the worker. The workers need to distinguish the needs of the individual from those who are disadvantaged by association and it is suggestive that the separate specialisations of boundary issues of 'who is the client' will require clarity in determining a course of planned intervention. The consequence of omitting a clear examination of the respective relationships and interactions might lead to a focus on either the individual or their immediate network of social and familial relationships.

Jason Mitchell (Burke, 1999), an individual with a mental health difficulty who was a restricted patient, was granted leave from hospital on the condition that he returned later in the day. This followed a period of good behaviour. However, instead of returning to hospital he travelled to his previous home and murdered a newly retired couple; a few days later, he murdered his father. Following an enquiry by Blom-Cooper (1996), management difficulties were indicated as a problem with the handling of the case although no blame was attached to the hospital staff. My own review of the case suggested that the 'locus of control' was partly to blame because the dangers to the family and public were not part of the understanding of Jason Mitchell's problems.

The issues which arise in this case are partly due to focusing only on the individual behaviour within the restricted environment of the hospital, and failing to recognise the difficulties within Jason Mitchell's circle of influence outside the hospital, which extended to the family and home environment. Once freed from the restrictions imposed within the regime of the hospital Jason Mitchell's previously controlled impulses were also released.

Broadening the focus from concern with the individual to one that was based on the family and community might have resulted in a better appreciation of the significance of removing restrictions on a dangerous individual. Although this is an extreme and violent example, and it is concerned more with dangerousness than disadvantage *per se*, it nevertheless serves the purpose of illustrating the importance of disadvantage, however constructed, to indicate the need for more extensive forms of assessment incorporating the ranges of social influence identified within Figure 10.1.

Equally, omitting the individual level of need in any assessment in order to focus more on family issues, or surrounding elements in the circle of influence, could have severe consequences if one failed to appreciate the individual perspective. It can also result in tragedy. Victoria Climbié was not seen by the social worker in the latter stages of her life because the worker accepted the views expressed by Victoria's aunt and partner that she was properly cared for when she was not. Victoria died and her aunt and partner were convicted of her murder. The enquiry by Lord Laming (2003) indicated a lack of information sharing and accountability and the fact that workers needed to build a 'fuller picture' rather than a 'snapshot' of the case in which they were involved. Not seeing Victoria during the later stages of her life meant that the picture that the worker viewed was not a reflection of the realities in the case.

The indications are that in both these cases, ignoring or not understanding the part of the system in which the individual or family was engaged could and did have dire consequences. Associative disadvantage would not in itself offer any solution to the problems that stem from individual difficulties and criminal actions, as indicated in the two cases mentioned above, which might not have been preventable. However, the questions and issues raised by these cases concern the nature of assessments when dealing with vulnerable or dangerous people; they reveal a need to examine the individual and those within the individual circle of interactions. The simple imperative of identifying child and adult needs, within the circle of the associative model, might clarify the fact that the focus has to be systematic, on the child or client and on the family. Assessment has to be at both levels, not one or the other: the system is holistic, it interacts, one impacts on the other, and that is the true nature of an ecological assessment. Any exclusion of such difficulties risks an assessment that produces an incomplete picture of need.

The level of worker engagement, in this system, should incorporate the individual, family and social systems that are involved. Disadvantage would seem a form of contagion in such circumstances as reported in the individual case examples provided, but its construction has social, situational and structural components, as these chapters have demonstrated. The consequence of such a construction has implications for practice and one way of addressing such needs is to reflect on what I have chosen to call the three 'Rs' of practice.

Rights, responsibilities and reflections: Back to the three 'Rs'
Rights
The concern for individual rights can be understood by looking at needs when making choices. Social work is largely defined, however, by the duties and responsibilities prescribed by the law, including the requirement of the Care Standards Act 2000, which prevents anyone calling themselves a social worker, and regulated by the General Social Care Council (2002), which provides registration of who is or is not a social worker. The intention here is not to provide a legal guide, although the essentials reflected upon link to the individual client and user and embrace the needs and rights of such individuals. The Human Rights Act 1998, therefore, is helpful in defining rights and identifies a full spectrum of human rights, applicable to all. These include the right to life, the right not to be tortured or experience inhuman and degrading treatment, the right not to be deprived of liberty, the right to private and family life and the right to not be discriminated against (Mandelstam, 2005). In assessing individual clients, social workers sometimes have to balance an individual's need for protection against their right to liberty, and in child care, this can result in a child's removal from home (Burke, 1999: 110). Barnes and Mercer (2003) express the view that rights involve recognition of choice and selection; clearly, any deprivation of individual rights would in fact appear to ignore the need for choice but may be justified when overriding that right for the client's or for the community's protection. The latter may be necessary for the safety of the individual who might be put at high levels of risk or for the safety of the public when the individual him- or herself is a source of danger. The latter is illustrated in the case of Jason Mitchell; had he not been released, as discussed above, he would not have been in the position to murder his father and an elderly couple.

In child care, the Children Act 1989 promotes child decision-making rights that require the child's view to be taken seriously (Fortin, 2003: 9) and so influences the situation and outcome decision reached when protection is an issue. The broader picture provided by Figure 10.1 would, in this child care illustration, also incorporate the views of the family in determining the outcome achieved. This should not, however, extend to the exclusion of the child as in Victoria Climbié's case and would suggest the need is to balance what is best for the child, give due consideration to his or her choice, and to recognise the risk within any situation, such that the latter is minimised. Indeed, as has previously been stated, in Victoria's case a full appreciation of the child's needs within the family context might have saved her life.

The right not to be discriminated against fits within the model of disadvantage by stigmatisation in recognising that individuals treated positively is required in *Valuing People* (Department of Health, 2004) where choice and opportunity for people with learning disabilities is advocated. The rights and obligations of local authorities to meet needs may come into conflict when needs as defined by the individual do not match those defined by the authority. Mandelstam (2005: 38) indicates that service users have few absolute legal rights or entitlements, such that legal resolution of cases in dispute often provides limited enforceable outcomes.

It appears, from this admittedly partial review, that legal rights are clear in principle but difficult to apply in practice due to the potential conflict of needs. The difficulties of disadvantage and stigmatisation arise as part of the human condition and identifying the role of the social worker, in promoting rights, through the empowerment of individuals within their circle of influence. In such circumstances, oppressive experiences need to be challenged as described in Chapter 9: not to do so perpetuates a sense of individual and social exclusion.

Responsibilities
Responsibilities might be considered to be about the enactment of rights but that is not the sense used here. Given our debate about disadvantage, the intent here is to reflect on professional responsibilities in terms of practice implications and the need to follow a code of practice governing professional conduct. Professional responsibilities, in this sense, would appear to lie between the provision of statutory services and the discretion of the worker in assessing the need for services (Smith, 2000: 272). Assessing need implies that the professional making the assessment acts responsibly and in doing so the ethical base of professional practice is applied. The ethics of practice will include, among others, respect for the client (or service user), honesty, collaboration with others, accountability and maintaining a creditable status (this is summarised by Clark, 2000). Of central importance to this discussion is the additional requirement that practice should be based on methods that are effective and helpful.

In a similar line of argument to my own about the need to consider the circle of influence, Dominelli (1997: 102) shows that not addressing racism directly blocks effective interactions between white social workers and black people and suggests that 'black people may pay with their lives'. She suggests that ignoring the problems of racism fails black people. Clearly the issue of professional responsibility must take account of cultural and racial differences: this fits very squarely with the sense that stigma blinds people to the problems of others, and it is why there is a need to acknowledge difference and diversity and to identify when such situations exist so that disadvantage is not the consequence.

Understanding difference and broadening our frame of perception and understanding is within the remit of professional responsibilities; to achieve that objective it is necessary to share decision-making processes with the individuals whose lives are subject to professional intervention. According to Hart (1992: 5) 'participation is the fundamental right of citizenship' or, as expounded by Miljeteig (2005: 129), responsibility taking involves participation in a form of partnership – it is about collaboration when working with others. This is exactly what professionals need to take account of when working with individuals and families, recognising the infrastructure and influences on people's lives, taking account of those elements (including vulnerability and the need for protection) and working together to achieve a desired outcome.

Reflections

In order to clarify the social work role, given recognition of the individual rights, their arena of involvements and the nature of interactions, and taking account of the worker's need to take responsibility for his or her actions, it helps to consider the process of reflection in professional activity. Fook (2004) indicates that in order to be effective in practice it is necessary to understand the power relationships between social structures.

In essence, the chapters in this text aim to understand such relationships through associative disadvantage, so that any potential failure of assessment is avoided when the 'ripple effect' of stigma is understood and the assessment process is inclusive of such a process. Indeed, the failures of practice highlighted in this chapter may have been understood more clearly if reflective practice had been used to consider the needs of the individual within the family and environmental framework. However, reflection on practice is usually associated with professional development, to clarify an understanding of experiences as a worker and 'honing skills and values for practice' (Horner, 2003: 9).

The process of critical reflection is about being intent on learning from experience and is concerned with self-evaluation, as clarified by Holland (2004): first, in a review of the worker's own constructions and assessments, and, second, as an evaluation of how clients or service users benefit from such interventions. In essence the client as consumer informs the practitioner about how his or her needs are being met (or not) and that enables the worker to consider the implications for future practice. Indeed, reflection in practice should serve to identify methods that are effective and helpful (Clark, 2000).

Experience in practice, according to Thompson (1995), has two forms: reflection in action that is about the ability to deal with situations as they happen, and reflection on action, which is learning from experience. Clearly, the latter will inform the former as the worker becomes more experienced. The practitioner should also bear in mind what Adams, Dominelli and Payne (2002: 335) refer to as the need for 'a more universal and less stigmatised service (health care and educations services) than social care has become'. However, it is clear from these chapters on disadvantage that practice is concerned with difficult and sometimes life-threatening situations, so the worker will need guidance and supervision to enable his or her practice to be effective and helpful, and will need to overcome any public perceptions that social care is less than its name might suggest. Stress may diminish the capacity to work effectively, so supervision is a necessary guide for the worker in dealing with any number of difficult situations.

Supervision may assist in making an assessment and reflecting on possible outcomes. Supervision should guide critical reflection and the maintaining of objectivity in the work environment (Baldwin, 2004). Supervision may be the responsibility of a line manager or specialist practitioner but should always enable a dialogue between the worker and someone in the agency with experience in the particular field of practice. The opportunity to reflect on the circle of influence, which has the potential to disadvantage the client, will enable an understanding of the difficulties experienced by the user or client and his or her own network, which supervision recognises also impacts on the worker (as Figure 10. 1 demonstrates). Critical thinking ensures practice reflects on experience, combined with theoretical understanding of the client and service user system, to develop the 'best evidence' (Trevithick, 2000: 170) and in understanding the system of associative disadvantage this text will take the reader a little beyond the more restricted frames of reference.

Conclusion
This book builds and broadens the sense of 'disability by association' into a much wider spectrum to reflect the sense of disadvantage experience across a range of client and user groups, including the impact on the worker. Disadvantage that distinguishes many individuals on the receiving end of

social work is associated with perceptions of need, identified by location, attitudes and barriers to change. A unifying framework of practice is concerned with the systematic understanding that disadvantage touches all in contact with it, irrespective of its formulation.

In this final chapter, the sense is that the tide of stigma influencing events sweeps across those in the immediate area of influence and is maintained by those choosing to be disassociated from the disadvantaged. The worker, in abstracting himself or herself from such a situation, is guided by the system framework of a holistic and ecological assessment, maintaining objectivity by considering the rights of the user, responsibilities of the worker and reflections on practice – achieving the three 'Rs' of practice. With luck, understanding social disadvantage and its associated consequences will help the worker clarify his or her role and responsibilities for the benefit of those on the receiving end of practice and those closest to it.

References

Adams, R., Dominelli, L. and Payne, M. (eds) (2002) *Social Work: Themes, Issues and Critical Debates.* Basingstoke: Palgrave.

Baldwin, M. (2004) 'Critical Reflection: Opportunities and Threats to Professional Learning and Service Development in Social Work Organisation.' In N. Gould and M. Baldwin (eds) *Social Work, Critical Reflections and the Learning Organisation.* Aldershot: Ashgate.

Barnes, C. and Mercer, G. (2003) *Disability.* Cambridge: Polity Press.

Blom-Cooper, L. (1996) *The Case of Jason Mitchell: Report of the Independent Committee of Inquiry.* London: Duckworth.

Burke, P. (1999) 'Social Service Staff: Risks they Face and their Dangerousness to Others.' In P. Parsloe (ed.) *Risk Assessment in Social Care and Social Work.* London: Jessica Kingsley Publishers.

Burke, P. and Montgomery, S. (2003) *Finding a Voice.* Birmingham: Ventura Press.

Clark, C. (2000) *Social Work Ethics: Politics, Principles and Practice.* Basingstoke: Macmillan.

Department of Health (2000) *Framework for the Assessment of Children in Need and their Families.* London: The Stationery Office.

Department of Health (2004) *Valuing People: Moving Forward Together. The Government's Annual Report on Learning Disability 2004.* London: The Stationery Office.

Dominelli, L. (1997) *Anti-Racist Social Work.* Basingstoke: Macmillan.

Donald, T. and Jureidini, J. (2004) 'Parenting capacity.' *Child Abuse Review 13,* 5–17.

Fook, J. (2004) 'Critical Reflection and Organisational Learning and Change.' In N. Gould and M. Baldwin (eds) *Social Work, Critical Reflection and the Learning Organisation.* Aldershot: Ashgate.

Fortin, J. (2003) *Children's Rights and the Developing Law.* 2nd edition. London: Lexis Nexis.

Garrett, P. (2003) 'Swimming with dolphins: the assessment framework, New Labour and new tools for social work with children and families.' *British Journal of Social Work 33,* 441–63.

General Social Care Council (2002) *Codes of Practice for Social Care Workers and Employers.* London: GSCC.

Hart, R. (1992) *Children's Participation: From Tokenism to Citizenship: Inocenti Essay No.4.* International Child Development Centre, Florence: UNICEF.

Holdsworth, L. (1991) *Empowerment Social Work with Physically Disabled People.* Norwich: Social Work Monographs.

Holland, S. (2004) *Child and Family Assessment in Social Work Practice*. London: Sage Publications.

Horner, N. (2003) *What is Social Work? Context and Perspectives*. London: Learning Matters.

Houston, S. (2002) 'Re-thinking a systemic approach to child welfare: a critical response to the framework for the assessment of children in need and their families.' *European Journal of Social Work 5*, 301–12.

Jack, G. (1997) 'An ecological approach to social work with children and families.' *Children and Family Social Work 2*, 109–20.

Laming, H. (2003) *The Victoria Climbié Inquiry Report*. Cm 5730. London: The Stationery Office, www.victoria-climbie-inquiry.org.uk (accessed March 2006).

Mandelstam, M. (2005) *Community Care Practice and the Law*. 3rd edition. London: Jessica Kingsley Publishers.

Miljeteig, P. (2005) 'Children's Democratic Rights: What We Can Learn From Young Workers Organizing Themselves.' In J. Mason and M. Fattore (eds) *Children Taken Seriously: In Theory, Policy and Practice*. London: Jessica Kingsley Publishers.

Powell, M. (2001) 'New Labour and the Third Way.' *Critical Social Policy 20*, 39–60.

Smith, C. (2000) 'Professional Discretion and Judicial Decision Making.' In M. Davies (ed.) *The Blackwell Encyclopaedia of Social Work*. Oxford: Blackwell Publishers.

Thompson, N. (1995) *Theory and Practice in Health and Social Welfare*. Buckingham: Open University Press.

Trevithick, P. (2000) *Social Work Skills: A Practice Handbook*. Buckingham: Open University Press.

The Contributors

Peter Burke is a senior lecturer in the Department of Social Work at the University of Hull. His work in disability-related research has, over the past 15 years, resulted in a number of texts, including the originating idea for this one, which extends the concepts and research presented in Peter's earlier book, *Brothers and Sisters of Disabled Children* (2004), also published by Jessica Kingsley Publishers.

Catherine Deverell has eight years of post-qualifying experience in child and family social work, some in voluntary sector family centres and the majority in statutory child care teams. She started working as a social work lecturer at the University of Hull in September 2003.

Benedict Fell is a qualified social worker and has experience of working with children and families and younger and older adults with mental health difficulties. Since 2003, he has been employed as a research assistant within the Faculty of Health and Social Care at the University of Hull on a number of projects. He is currently working as a lecturer in the Department of Social Work at the University of Hull and is studying for an MPhil in social work.

Philip Guy is lecturer in addictions at the University of Hull. He has been involved with the health and welfare of drug users for over 20 years. Philip's research interests include family aspects of substance use and the cultural representation of drug users.

Margaret Holloway is Professor of Social Work at the University of Hull. She retains an interest in social work practice in palliative care and bereavement and loss. Her particular interest is in Parkinson's disease and for some years she served on the research advisory panels of the Parkinson's Disease Society, UK. Margaret is also pursuing work with clinicians in neurology on the implementation of a user-led care pathway for people with Parkinson's disease and their carers.

Jonathan Parker is Professor of Social Work at Bournemouth University. He has written extensively on social work education, practice learning, dementia and the social work process. He is series editor of the successful *Transforming Social Work Practice* series.

Elizabeth Price is a lecturer in social work at the University of Hull. Her background is in adult mental health services. Prior to training as a social worker, she spent many years working in the NHS with adults with enduring mental health problems. Later, as a specialist social worker, she worked primarily with older people who had a diagnosis of dementia. Elizabeth's current research interests include the experiences of gay and lesbian carers of people with dementia, and policy and practice-related issues for gay and lesbian foster carers.

Liz Walker is Senior Lecturer in the Department of Social Work, University of Hull, and research associate at the Wits Institute for Social and Economic Research, University of the Witwatersrand, Johannesburg. She is co-editor of *Men Behaving Differently, South African Men since 1994* (2005, Double Storey Books) and co-author of *Waiting to Happen: HIV/AIDS in South Africa* (2004, Lynne Rienner Publishers).

Subject Index

Author Index

DATE DUE

DEC 31 '08 R

DEC 0 8 2008

GAYLORD   PRINTED IN U.S.A.